VICTORIAN PUBLISHERS' BOOK-BINDINGS
IN PAPER

for
RACHEL *and* SARAH
and their parents

The Children's Picture Gallery
No imprint, 1859
302 × 232 mm

Foreword signed J. C. (Joseph Cundall): basically the same book
as *Cabinet Pictures by Modern Painters*, published by Cundall, 1862.
Paper on cloth boards, printed in colours from wood by Leighton
Bros, design signed Albert H. Warren. ECB: 8*s.*6*d*, Leighton, 1859.
Upper cover is shown on p.3; the illustration in the roundel on the
upper cover is shown above.
Massey College, Toronto, JC139

THE CHILDREN'S PICTURE GALLERY

ENGRAVINGS FROM
ONE HUNDRED PAINTINGS
BY EMINENT ENGLISH ARTISTS
ADAPTED FOR THE YOUNG

Ruari McLean

VICTORIAN

PUBLISHERS'

BOOK-BINDINGS

IN PAPER

Berkeley and Los Angeles
UNIVERSITY OF CALIFORNIA PRESS
1983

First published in the USA in 1983 by
University of California Press, Berkeley and Los Angeles
First published in the United Kingdom in 1983 by
The Gordon Fraser Gallery Ltd, London and Bedford
Copyright © Ruari McLean 1983

The illustrations for the binding
were drawn by JOHN LAWRENCE

Printed at The Roundwood Press, Kineton, Warwick,
England
Bound by Pitman Press, Bath

Library of Congress Catalogue Card Number: 83-40019

ISBN 0-520-05102-5

Contents

'Common or garden bindings'
The literature of bibliography and book-collecting is enormous.
There is not one aspect of it, you would think, on which a dozen
or more standard works had not appeared in the last half-century,
besides a vast number of articles, appendices and so forth in general
works and periodicals. You would think so, and you would be
wrong. Almost everyone who writes about these things is concerned
with the inside of the book; and of the few who are interested in
its outside, almost all restrict their interest to such glorious exteriors
as were imposed upon books by Clovis Eve and Derome and their
kind. The literature of common or garden bindings, original
bindings, publishers' bindings, could be carried comfortably in the
pockets of a roomy overcoat.

From John Carter's *Binding Variants in English Publishing 1820-1900*,
as entertaining and invaluable today as when first published fifty
years ago, – and, incidentally, issued in marbled paper on boards.

Bibliography

MAME ET FILS. *Alfred Mame & Fils à Tours: Notice et Spécimens.* Tours, 1867

ARSÈNE ALEXANDRE, M. H. SPIELMANN, H. C. BUNNER & A. JACCACI. *The Modern Poster,* New York, 1895

PERCIVAL POLLARD. *Posters in Miniature.* New York & London, 1896

BRANDER MATTHEWS. *Bookbindings Old and New* (with section on bindings in paper). Bell, 1896

OCTAVE UZANNE. *L'Art dans la Decoration Exterieure des Livres en France et à l'Etranger.* Paris, 1898

ESTHER WOOD, & OTHERS. *Modern Book Bindings & their designers.* Winter Number of *The Studio,* London 1899

GUMUCHIAN ET CIE. *Les Livres de l'Enfance.* 2 vols, Paris, n.d. [1930]

MICHAEL SADLEIR. *The Evolution of Publishers' Binding Styles 1770-1900,* Constable, 1930

JOHN CARTER. *Binding Variants in English Publishing 1820-1900* Constable, 1932

JOSEPH W. ROGERS, 'The Industrialization of American Bookbinding', in *Gutenberg Jahrbuch,* Mainz, 1938

PICKERING & CHATTO. *The Victorian Novel 1837-1901 An illustrated catalogue of a unique Collection of Victorian Fiction (Three-Deckers to Yellow-Backs) mostly in fine original condition.* Pickering and Chatto Ltd, c.1939

NICOLAS RAUCH. 'Les Livres de l'époque Romantique' in *Formes et Couleurs,* nos 3/4. Paris, 1945

JEAN ADHÉMAR. 'Le Livre Romantique' in *Portique* no.5, Paris, 1947

R. BRUN. *Le Livre Français.* Paris, 1948

L-M. MICHON. *La Reliure Française.* Paris, 1951

The History of Bookbinding 525-1950 AD. Exhibition Catalogue, Baltimore, Maryland, 1957

TORONTO PUBLIC LIBRARY. *The Osborne Collection of Early Children's Books.* Vol I, 1958 and Vol II, 1975.

ALBERT HAEMMERLE. *Buntpapier.* Munich, 1961

BERNARD MIDDLETON. *A History of English Craft Bookbinding Technique.* New York, 1963

ROBERT METZDORF. 'Victorian Book Decoration' in *The Princeton University Chronicle,* vol. XXIV no.2, Winter 1963 (illustrated)

ANNE RENIER. *Friendship's Offering.* Private Libraries Association, 1964

J. ADHÉMAR & J. P. SEQUIN. *Le Livre Romantique.* Paris, 1968

GORDON N. RAY. *Victoria R.I.* Bookseller's catalogue, 3 vols., issued by David Magee, San Francisco, 1969*

E. & E. PINTO. *Tunbridge and Scottish Souvenir Woodware.* Bell, 1970

PETER A. WICK (editor). *The Turn of the Century: 1885-1910.* Art Nouveau – Jugendstil Books, Houghton Library, Harvard University 1970

FRANK E. COMPARATO. *Books for the Million.* Harrisburg, Penn., 1971

PHILIP GASKELL. *A New Introduction to Bibliography.* Oxford, 1972

PETER A. WICK (editor). *Toulouse-Lautrec Book Covers and Brochures.* Harvard College Library 1972

F. W. FAXON. *Literary Annuals and Gift Books, a Bibliography 1823-1903.* Reprinted with supplementary essays by Eleanore Jamieson & Iain Bain. Private Libraries Association, 1973

ERIC QUAYLE. *The Collector's Book of Books.* London, 1971

The Collector's Book of Children's Books. London, 1971

MICHAEL SADLEIR. 'Aspects of the Victorian Novel' in *Publishing History* V, 1979

GEOFFREY PERKINS. *George Auriol: a catalogue of graphic work.* Bookseller's catalogue issued by Christopher Drake and Warrack & Perkins, 1982

F. J. HARVEY DARTON. *Children's Books in England,* 3rd edn. Cambridge, 1982

*This collection was bought in its entirety by Brigham Young University, Provo, Utah, U.S.A.

Foreword

The main purpose of the present work is to show, by illustration, some of the attractive ways that paper was used as the main surface on publishers' bindings between – roughly speaking – 1800 and 1900.

Paper was the cheapest binding material and since it could be printed on by any process in any number of colours, it gave almost unlimited freedom to designers; but there was a price paid in durability: paper was easier to damage or wear out, and more difficult to repair, than any of the other materials used. Therefore, comparatively few examples of books in paper bindings have survived in anything like the glamorous condition in which many of them were originally issued. I have been lucky in finding a few examples in almost pristine condition to photograph for this book; many are positively shabby, but each of these may be, for all I know, the only or the best surviving copy of this binding in the world, and thus worth showing *faute de mieux*. I know of no public collection that specializes in this aspect of book design, but some may exist.* Until recently, most libraries receiving books bound in paper had them automatically rebound or re-covered in something stronger – and have only recently recognized this as occasionally amounting to vandalism.

I have already illustrated (both in colour and black and white) some fine examples of Victorian publishers' bindings in paper in *Victorian Book Design* (2nd edn, 1972) and in *Joseph Cundall* (Private Libraries Association, 1976); I have therefore tried to avoid duplication, by not allowing the same reproductions to appear in the present work. The only repetition is of the papier-mâché bindings shown in *Victorian Book Design;* in the present volume, I reproduce *all* the papier-mâché bindings known to me to exist. If anyone knows of any others, I will be most grateful to learn of them.

In all cases, unless there is evidence to the contrary, it is assumed that the date of publication is the date of the binding illustrated. Where the date of publication appears in square brackets [], it means that the book carried no publication date, and has been given this date in the British Library Catalogue, the English Catalogue of Books, or other source quoted. It is to be remembered that gift books bearing a date on the title page were generally on sale in time for Christmas of the previous year.

All books captioned as belonging to 'Massey College, Toronto', are from the Ruari McLean Collection, and are reproduced here by permission of the Master and Fellows of Massey College in the University of Toronto.

Measurements, in millimetres, are of the outside of the case, the width taken to the hinge of the spine as accurately as possible.

The following abbreviations have been used:

VBD	*Victorian Book Design and Colour Printing,* 2nd edition, 1972
VPBCL	*Victorian Publishers' Book-Bindings in Cloth and Leather,* 1974
ECB	*English Catalogue of Books*
BN	*Bibliothèque Nationale,* Paris, *Catalogue of Books*

Acknowledgements

I am deeply grateful to various friends for the loan of many of the books, all rare and precious, illustrated in this volume: without their generosity, it could hardly have been produced. These friends include Robin de Beaumont, Fianach Lawry, Bernard Middleton, Don Parkinson, John Porter, Nigel Temple, and the late Percival Hinton,

*There are, of course, small or not so small collections of books bound in paper in many libraries, for example the V. & A. Museum Library in London, the Rare Book Dept. in the Houghton Library of Harvard University in Cambridge, Mass., and the Brigham Young University, Utah, but it is rare for them to be specially collected or housed together.

who sadly died while the work was in preparation. To Sue Allen, Rodney Engen, Colin Franklin, Eric Quayle, Vivian Ridler, John Saumarez-Smith, Hans Schmoller, and Professor Michael Twyman I am most grateful for providing photographs and information.

For advice and information, I am grateful to the British, Victoria and Albert, Bodleian and St Bride's Libraries, the Pepys Library in Magdalene College, Cambridge, the National Library of Scotland, the Osborne Collection of Early Children's Books in Toronto Public Library and the Houghton Library in Harvard University, Cambridge, Mass.; and, as individuals, to Mirjam Foot, Howard Nixon, Irene Whalley, Michael Darby, James Mosley, R. C. Latham, John Morris, Margaret Crawford Maloney and Eleanor M. Garvey. I am also most grateful to Dr Desmond Neill, Librarian of Massey College in the University of Toronto, for providing colour transparencies, which were taken by Karen Hendrik of Toronto, of books in the Ruari McLean Collection under his care; he also checked my descriptions of the books, and gave me valuable bibliographical advice. Simon Nowell-Smith made helpful suggestions on my text; and Professor A. S. G. Curtis analysed a broken papier-mâché binding and confirmed that it was made of a mixture of plaster on a papier-mâché (i.e. fibrous) base.

I am grateful to David Lloyd of London for his care and skill in taking the bulk of the photographs in this volume. Peter Guy and Simon Kingston of Gordon Fraser have afforded continuous help and encouragement.

Valerie Toon typed most of my text more times than I want to remember; and without my wife, I could never have finished the book or survived a move from Dollar to the island of Mull that we undertook in the middle of writing it.

RUARI McLEAN
Carsaig, Isle of Mull

'OLD METHOD OF ROUNDING BOOKS.

Introduction

Printing needs paper: it is therefore an essential ingredient of a book. Paper was used for covering books, as well as for printing them, from the earliest days. Vellum and leather were more durable as binding materials, but paper was cheaper. It was used, in single or double sheets, or pasted on card or board, to protect a book until the book found an owner who could afford to bind it properly in leather.

For many years, publishing as we think of it today did not exist as a separate profession: printing, publishing and bookselling overlapped and were often carried out by the same man or firm. But during the eighteenth century in Britain, publishing firms were founded whose names still exist in modern publishing: Rivington in 1711, Longman in 1724, John Murray in 1768, Constable and Nelson before 1800. Their books were normally issued either bound in plain leather – calf or sheepskin – or in plain (usually brown) paper pasted on boards. There was often no identification on the paper spine, or else the title was written, either directly on the spine, or on a pasted-on label. Then it was printed on a white paper label, and eventually, spare labels were included inside, printed on the last sheet of the book. These bindings were clearly thought of as temporary, for books that were intended, on purchase, to be bound in leather to the purchaser's specification. These were substantial, serious books, works of literature. Pamphlets and children's books were slighter, and had different treatment. It would be natural to print the title of a pamphlet on its paper cover, whether it was plain, the same as the text, or coloured; children's books, usually smaller than other books, were often bound in 'flowery and gilt' paper (cf. Philip James, *Children's Books of Yesterday*, 1933, pp. 21, 24). These patterned papers, also known as 'Dutch gilt' or 'Dutch flowery', were mostly produced in Augsburg, Furth, and Nurnberg in Germany, and also in Italy, and are described, with illustrations in colour, in Albert Haemmerle's *Buntpapier* ('Decorated paper'), Munich, 1961. The name 'Dutch' may derive from 'Deutsch' ('German') or from the fact that the papers were imported through Holland – as were also 'marbled' papers, patterned by transfer from colours floating on a solution of size, an ancient process that may have originated in Japan and was used for end-papers by fifteenth-century Persian book artists. Dutch gilt, marbled, and other patterned papers were used by binders in Britain throughout the seventeenth, eighteenth and nineteenth centuries for end-papers and for covering books, pamphlets and music: there are several examples in Samuel Pepys' Library in Magdalene College, Cambridge. An example is shown on p.17.

It would also be natural to print a block on the cover of a book for children, and an example of this – a genuine 'publisher's binding' – is shown on p.18, dated 1785: no doubt much earlier examples exist.

*The Infant's Library, c.*1800, shown on p.19, was a series of tiny books bound in different coloured papers, with cut-out oval printed labels pasted down on front and back. The little books on religious subjects shown on the same page, produced probably in 1840, were not children's books, but intended for working folk who did not have much money to spend. The simple patterned papers in which they are covered could probably be bought in stationers' shops (at several sheets for a farthing?). These are the earliest examples I know of patterned papers used in Britain by a publisher (who was also a printer) for an edition not intended for children.

The practice of printing the title of a book or booklet on its front paper cover does not seem to have become usual until early in the nineteenth century. Sometimes a printer merely repeated the title-page, but by the 1820s covers were being designed as covers, with the

An early Italian patterned paper, printed from wood in various colours.

Poems by the Rev. George Crabbe
Printed for J. Hatchard, 1809
4th edition, 2 vols
185 × 110 mm

Blue paper spine with printed paper labels stuck on; pink paper on boards.
Collection the late Percival Hinton

The Amulet
1828 (see p.24)

The carton, with printed design
pasted on side.
Massey College, Toronto, PB68

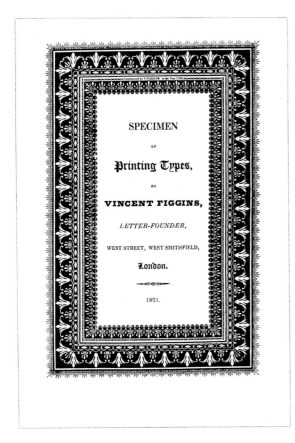

The title-page of Vincent Figgins'
Specimen of 1821; but his rich borders
were seldom used by contemporary
publishers in books in this way.

title also on the spine, showing that such books were expected to stand on bookshelves. The usual practice was to set the wording of the title, author, etc. inside a tasteful woodcut or typographical border, and this was done by provincial presses all over Britain. Examples are shown on pp. 20-22. The style continued to be used, on substantial paper-on-boards bindings, throughout the nineteenth century, presumably as a less expensive, yet tasteful, alternative to cloth (which had been introduced in London as a commercial binding material for books in the mid 1820s).

The next step was to abandon type, and draw a cover design, which would have to be etched on copper, cut on wood, or drawn on a lithographic stone.

It was in fact the Annuals – small gift books designed for ladies to carry in their reticules – which first showed the full design potentialities of paper as a binding material. Their history has been engagingly sketched by Mrs Anne Renier in a booklet, *Friendship's Offering,* published by the Private Libraries Association in 1964, and further documented in F. W. Faxon's *Literary Annuals and Gift Books,* reprinted by the P.L.A. in 1973. The Annuals were started in Britain by Rudolph Ackermann, copying the Annuals that he remembered as being so successful on the Continent. They were issued before Christmas, but were given the following year's date: *i.e.* an Annual dated 1822 on the title-page was issued in 1821. They were intended principally for ladies, young or otherwise, and contained stories, poems, illustrations and sometimes music, elegantly packaged. The bindings were always elaborately decorative. Whether the book itself was bound in leather gilt, crimson watered silk, peacock's feathers or paper, it was often enclosed in a slip-case, which can be called the progenitor of the bookjacket, since its function was to attract and protect. Examples are shown on pp.24-5. Ackermann's first Annual, the *Forget Me Not,* was published in 1821: the first one for children appeared in 1827, when Westley & Davies cashed in on Ackermann's title with *The Juvenile Forget Me Not;* Ackermann came back with *Ackermann's Juvenile Forget Me Not,* in 1829. The cover for Ackermann's second *Juvenile Forget Me Not,* shown on p.25, raises a question that recurs again and again in our pages: it is a lovely design, but did it appeal to children? It seems a long way removed in spirit from the gaiety of Cruikshank's illustrations for the translations of stories by the Brothers Grimm, first published in London in 1823: but what we must call over-sophisticated adult design remains a feature of nineteenth-century children's book covers for at least half the century.

Queen Victoria came to the throne in 1837, twenty-two years after the defeat of Napoleon at Waterloo. It was a period of enormous expansion for Britain, in terms especially of population and wealth: coal, steam, the railways, etc., etc. This expansion was actively reflected and promoted by the printing industry. In 1814, *The Times* in London became the first newspaper in the world to be printed on a steam-driven cylinder machine instead of a hand press. Although the invention was a German's, he had to come to London to exploit it. In 1821, Vincent Figgins, a London type-founder, issued a specimen book of types and decorative borders which shows some of the visual richness then being made available to express the dignity, ebullience, pomposity and good taste, backed by money, then requiring expression. Figgins's borders were not much used in books, but they were used on the covers of books issued in parts, and for many kinds of ephemeral printing and publicity, and continue to be used by typographers of today.

The Victorian period gradually – some would say swiftly – took on its own shape and character. The Great Exhibition of 1851 was a monumental expression of it in visual terms; how we wish that we, today, could have walked though the aisles of the Crystal Palace! The wood-engravings of the catalogues and the *Art-Journal,* the colour prints of Baxter, Leighton and Dickinson, the chromolithographs of Digby Wyatt, give us only a faint idea of what it must have been like. Many of the exhibits we might deplore, but there was also much of beauty, as surviving steam engines and other machinery of the mid-Victorian period can show. The profession of 'designer' did not then exist: 'design' was mostly done, well or ill, by the craftsman with traditional tools: the trouble came when he was superseded by a machine.

In the design of book covers, and other forms of graphic design, we can see the gradual emergence of the professional designer, perhaps earlier than elsewhere. The most notable example is in the career of Owen Jones (1809-74), an architect by training, who was entrusted with designing the colour scheme for the interior of the Great Exhibition in 1851. He found that the new art of chromolithography was the only practicable way to publish the measured drawings he had made in colour of the Alhambra Palace. He set up his own lithographic printing press to carry this out, became a pioneer of chromolithographic illustration as a tool for art education (his *Grammar of Ornament,* first published in 1856, and republished throughout the century, was a mainstay of nearly every architect's office in the country until well into the present century); he designed and illustrated many books of his own; and finally hired out his skills as a graphic designer to other publishers, to the printing firm of De la Rue, for whom he designed advertisements, packaging, and the decorative backs of playing cards, and to Huntley & Palmer, for whom he designed a famous biscuit tin. A biography of Jones is badly needed, but until it appears, examples of his work can be studied in my *Victorian Book Design and Colour Printing,* 2nd edn, 1972, and book covers designed by him are shown here on pp.30, 33, 49. His influence on other designers and publishers was considerable.

Another influence was the work of the antiquary Henry Shaw (1800-73). He was the author of a series of books of plates describing medieval and Elizabethan art and architecture and the art of the illuminated manuscript: he was a skilful draughtsman and faithful copier, rather than a creative designer. Most of his books were published by William Pickering, supported by the distinguished typography and printing of the Chiswick Press. The Grolier and other strap-work designs reproduced in his *Encyclopedia of Ornament,* 1842, provided a theme that recurs on book covers throughout our period (cf. pp.11, 44, 45). The so-called 'Erasmus pattern', which he illustrated in colour as plate 6 of the *Encyclopedia,* was copied almost exactly, but slightly simplified, on *The Poets' Pleasaunce,* 1847, shown on p.31. In a paper entitled 'On Ornamental Art applied to ancient and modern bookbinding' read by Joseph Cundall to the Society of Arts in November 1847, Cundall, talking about 'revival patterns', starts off with the Erasmus pattern, commenting first that it was 'much more beautifully executed' in Shaw's book, and then that

this is the fourth time this design has been borrowed within five years, so we must conclude that there is a real excellence about it. But why should it have been chosen to decorate a book outside, which is so differently, and at the same time, so beautifully ornamented within; there, flower borders of a luxuriant richness surround many of the pages; while outside, there are a series of lines which are not in the least in harmony or keeping. What a chance was here lost of giving an appropriate and really beautiful new binding.

This might have been a designer's thoughts today, as well as nearly 150 years ago. Cundall also comments, with approval, on the paper 'which *Lady Willoughby* wears', which we show on p.36: and ends, 'Let us hope, then, that it will not be long ere such original Ornamental Art shall be wedded to our present perfect execution, that the nineteenth century will be able, like the fifteenth, to boast a style of

Some of Vincent Figgins' borders, mostly from his *Specimen* of 1833.

Gracefulness etc.
ed. Arthur Freeling
Houlston & Stoneman, n.d.
[between 1844 and 1847]
125 × 76 mm

Paper on cloth on boards, printed from wood (? by Gregory, Collins & Reynolds), in red, blue and gold. A variation of the strapwork theme.
Collection R. de Beaumont

Sketches of Young Ladies, etc.
by 'Quiz', with six illustrations by
'Phiz'
Chapman & Hall, n.d. (inscribed
1837)
164 × 102 mm

White or grey card printed in black
from wood, signed 'Phiz. del., E.
Landells sc.' Price one shilling. The
title is printed on the spine, running
upwards.

its own.' This pious hope was not, I think, fulfilled.

The other well-known example of an 'artist' who became a 'designer' is John Leighton (1822-1912), who used the pseudonym 'Luke Limner' and specialized in drawing the designs which were cut in brass and stamped in gold on publisher's cloth and leather bindings, the subject of my earlier book in this series. An example of his work on paper covers is shown here on p.64. John Leighton, and his family, active and distinguished particularly in colour printing and bookbinding, are another case of a subject, or subjects, in search of an author.

Two of the most sensational bookbinding designs of the period before 1851, on paper (not illustrated here because I have already illustrated them in colour in *Victorian Book Design*) are *The Illuminated Calendar*, 1845 and *The Art of Illumination and Missal Painting*, 1849. Both are presumed to have been designed by H. Noel Humphreys, because he was the author-illustrator in both cases of the book itself. Another similar example, illustrated here on p.32, is Joseph Cundall's *A Booke of Christmas Carols*, 1845. These designs all involved embossing, as well as rich colour against a background of white and gold, and seem to owe some inspiration to a style then current in France, known today as 'cartonnage romantique'.

French Romantic Bindings

Examples of these French 'romantic bindings' are shewn on pp. 46-8. This kind of binding was widely used in France for a long period, perhaps mainly for books designed to be awarded as school prizes. They were issued in long series and appear to be intended to give instruction rather than entertainment. They were far prettier than the similar 'improving' books being issued in paper on boards at the same time in Britain by Chambers, Nelson, Collins and others (cf. pp. 36, 60); but they were more fragile.

Their construction, whereby the central panel on the front was often cut out, and the whole cover laid over a colour plate pasted down separately on the boards, seems to be unnecessarily complicated: one wonders why the central illustration was not printed on the same paper. The economical French must have had a reason for this practice.

I have been unable to find in France either a public collection of these delightful bindings or any book about them. *Le Livre Romantique*, by Jean Adhémar and Jean-Pierre Sequin, Paris 1968, was published as a gift for friends of the Crédit Lyonnais and cannot be bought – except if a copy comes on the antiquarian market: it is more concerned with 'romantic' book illustration, but does illustrate two beautiful romantic paper bindings, *Hommage aux demoiselles*, 1819, and *Hommage aux dames*, 1828, and another dated 1837. These seem to have been in the gift-book class. The periodical *Arts et Métiers Graphiques*, in no.18 of 15 July 1930, published a short article 'Sur les cartonnages de l'époque romantique' with a colour plate showing 4 examples, of which two are closely similar to our own examples. Gumuchian's famous catalogue *Les Livres de l'Enfance* includes a special section on 'Cartonnages Romantiques', with many reproductions of these fascinating covers in black and white, and a frontispiece to each volume in colour. Not all the books illustrated and described seem to have been specifically intended for children. The insides were dull, occasionally illustrated with a few steel engravings, but never, so far as I know, with colour.

Papier-mâché

The 'illuminated' gift books which became a feature of British publishing during the 1840s were essentially gift books whose text was often, but not always, taken from the Bible, and whose pages were decorated in colour in a style closely or distantly resembling that of a medieval manuscript. They were usually printed by chromolithography, which Owen Jones had pioneered in Britain, and Owen Jones and Henry Noel Humphreys were for some years the two leading artist-producers of illuminated books. As much care was taken with the bindings of these books as with their insides, and many of them were issued in a variety of binding styles. Sometimes the same design was blocked in gold, or in blind, on different materials; often, both the design and the materials were totally different. Perhaps strangest of all were the papier-mâché bindings. The process was apparently invented by Messrs Jackson & Son of 49 Rathbone Place, whose name is given as the manufacturers in the Great Exhibition Catalogue, Class 17, under 'Leighton, Jane and Robert' (the bookbinders). The design was carved in a mould (of steel?), into which was poured a mixture of plaster on a papier-mâché base. The binding was usually strengthened by a metal armature. The composition sides were usually hinged on leather spines, but in some cases the spine also was made of papier-mâché. All the papier-mâché bindings that I have seen are black except that on *Quarles' Emblems,* 1845, (p.50), which is brown. The covers for this book were cast from the same moulds as were used for the Bible dated 1843, illustrated also on p.50.

The earliest date on a book with a papier-mâché binding is 1843, but that does not mean that the date of issue of copies in papier-mâché was 1843; sheets with that date could have been bound at any later date. In 1847, Longman published two illuminated books, *The Parables of Our Lord,* illuminated by H. Noel Humphreys, and *The Good Shunamite,* illuminated by Lewis Gruner, both of which appeared in papier-mâché in the year of publication; copies of *The Parables of Our Lord* were also issued in a leather binding by Hayday.

Joseph Cundall, in the paper to the Society of Arts quoted above, calls papier-mâché 'the monastic style', and said of it 'such covers can only be executed when great numbers are required, as they are cast in moulds, the first cost of which is very great'. Probably the usual quantity for a papier-mâché binding was 1000. It is worth noticing that two of the papier-mâché bindings shown were later adapted for other titles. The Great Exhibition catalogue describes them as 'in imitation of carved ebony', which seems unlikely: the inspiration more probably came either from medieval book covers in wood, ivory or metal (although no actual model is known) or the carving on, for example, cathedral choir stalls: the actual designs of papier-mâché covers seem to be entirely original. They are part of the Victorian Gothic revival, or dream of medievalism, to be placed reverently on a velvet cloth on the piano. They do not stand comfortably on shelves. Collectors today usually make boxes for them. They were originally sold in simple coloured paper-covered cartons, a few of which have survived.

Besides papier-mâché, the Victorians produced various other fancy bindings for gift books, more remarkable perhaps for their ingenuity than for either beauty or taste. Some bindings were hand-made, whether carved in wood (see VPBCL, p.48) or made out of other materials, and even if made in quantity, it is difficult to accept them as true examples of publishers' bindings. *The Preacher,* illuminated by Owen Jones, appeared in 1849 in a binding* imitating a carved wood binding, which was actually stamped out of wood, and it is the only specimen of that process that I have seen. I illustrated, in *Victorian Publishers' Bookbindings in Cloth and Leather,* some examples of 'mauchline ware' bindings (pp.48-9) and have shown some more here, together with Paul Jerrard's and other comparable bindings, on pp.72-74, since in most of them paper was required for the printing of an image. Mauchline ware was wood (usually sycamore); when used for binding a book, the back was often left as a varnished veneer or plain wood surface, while the front often bore a sheet of pasted-down paper,

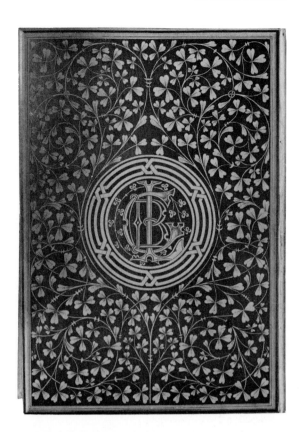

Moore's Irish Melodies
1846
The lower side of the cover shown on p.30, probably by Owen Jones.
Collection R. de Beaumont

* Illustrated in VBD, p.95.

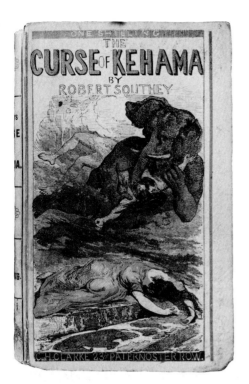

The Curse of Kehama
R. Southey
H. Vizetelly & Clarke, Beeton &
Co., 1853
170 × 105 mm

Yellow paper on boards printed in
red and dark blue by Jas Wade.
Collection R. de Beaumont

Chats by the Sea
James Clarke, 1868
162 × 102 mm

Pink paper on boards printed from
wood and type in red, blue and black.
Collection R. de Beaumont

printed with a tartan or other colour-printed image, or a steel engraving; the process by which this was transferred onto the wood is given by Edward and Eva Pinto, *Tunbridge and Scottish Souvenir Woodware*, Bell, 1970: 'The method of transferring was, first, to coat the box with two or three coats of shellac and the face of the print was also varnished. The print was then put ink side downwards on the object being decorated, and left to dry, which took one to two hours. The print was then sponged and the Japanese paper was rubbed off with a damp cloth'. When photographs were used on Mauchline bindings, they had to be pasted down as cut-outs.

Paul Jerrard's so-called 'porcelain' bindings were, I believe, made of a plaster composition similar to the papier-mâché bindings, which was then treated with a varnish, probably shellac. This surface could be blocked in gold, like cloth or leather.

Another fashion of the sixties and seventies was to simulate precious medieval bindings by means of brass edging, sometimes with clasps (see p.74): oddly enough, this seems to have been done only on cheaply printed books.

Children's Books

Although colour printing, both from wood and metal blocks and by chromolithography, had been used for children's books from the 1840s, children's books continued to be published with hand-coloured plates for many years. It was not until the 1860s that large-scale production of children's books printed in colour really began. In 1865 Frederic Warne, who had been George Routledge's partner from 1851, set up on his own, and both Warne and Routledge began publishing the paperback Toy Books which became one of the most attractive features of British publishing for the next 20 or 30 years. I have devoted some dozen pages to reproductions of their covers here and would like to devote a whole book to them. Their covers were designed in many styles; many were pictorial, but the ones that seem to me most beautiful and characteristic are those with 'fairground' lettering and decoration. Whether fairground, farmcart and narrow-boat decoration and lettering did actually provide the first inspiration, and if so, who the genius was that first seized on it for these covers, I cannot say, but I can think of no other source. The lettering and borders, which are essentially expressed in colours, did not come out of the typefounders' specimen books. They have a marvellous verve and vitality and they are purely decorative, with no visual connection of any kind with either the text or the illustrations inside. Routledge's and Warne's various series, of which Warne's 'Aunt Louisa Toy Books' were perhaps the most popular, had a rigid formula of coloured covers, eight pages of plain type matter printed in black, and eight pages of illustrations printed in four or more colours. Colour was the predominant feature of the books: very few appeared with black and white illustrations, even on the text pages, and I have seen only one that was 'landscape' in format. Illustrators of the earliest Aunt Louisas were named as H. S. Marks, J. D. Watson, Pickersgill, Harrison Weir, and F. Keyl; but soon the illustrators' names were dropped from the covers, and the drawings were mostly unsigned. The drawing was usually unpretentious but down-to-earth, and vigorous; I think that they owed a great deal to the engraving and colour-printing firms, (principally Edmund Evans, Kronheim, Leighton, Vincent Brooks, Dickes and Dalziel) who often, if not always, commissioned the artists.

It was Edmund Evans, the printer and wood-engraver, who created the most famous Toy Books of all, by commissioning first the young Walter Crane, then Randolph Caldecott, and finally Kate Greenaway, although Kate Greenaway's books were mostly produced in hard covers, so were not Toy Books in the accepted meaning of the words.

In the 1880s, the character of illustrated children's books in Britain seems to change, and it is not a change, artistically speaking, for the better. There seem to be more and more wishy-washy books published by Ernest Nister and Raphael Tuck, mostly printed by chromolithography in Bavaria. Much of the artwork for these books and their bindings is by unnamed artists without much character – it contrasts unfavourably with the work of Crane, Caldecott and Greenaway which was still being sold all this time.

At the same time, some very ingenious and amusing 'pop-up' and other books with moving parts were published, for which there is a revival at the present time, a hundred years later. Another new fashion was for 'shaped' books: four are shown on p.97. These are areas where books merge into toys – and fascinating areas they are, but beyond our province here.

Fin-de-Siècle and Art Nouveau

In an amusing and perceptive essay on 'Victorian Book Decoration', published in *The Princeton University Library Chronicle* (vol. XXIV, no.2, Winter 1963) the late Robert Metzdorf wrote 'It should not be imagined that the members of the Stationers' Company, their employees, sub-contractors, and artists gathered together in London on the morning of June 20th in 1837 and were thus addressed by the Worshipful Master: "Gentlemen: England has a new Queen whose name, it appears, is Victoria. From this moment forth we will design Victorian books".' In the same way, it must not be imagined that towards the end of the century, artists and designers suddenly decided to design only fin-de-siècle or art nouveau books – although in fact it does look so much as if that is what happened.

There were two obvious 'movements' that heralded changes in design in England: one was the arts-and-crafts movement, of which the Kelmscott Press, founded by William Morris in 1891, was most influential, although Morris was essentially a medievalist; the other was 'Art Nouveau', whose first manifestation in England is said to have been the often-reproduced title-page of A. H. MackMurdo's *Wren's City Churches,* 1883. Maurice Rheims in *The Age of Art Nouveau,* 1966, says that Art Nouveau was essentially 'forward-looking'. Whatever the labels, it is certain that new and exciting ideas in design became evident during the 1890s all over Europe and in the United States. An area in which this can be seen most clearly is in the new field of poster design – which had a strong influence on magazine and book covers. This was noticed in *The Modern Poster,* a book published in New York by Charles Scribner's Sons in 1895. The first chapter, written by Arsène Alexandre, is entitled 'French posters and book covers', and gives an amusing account of how the book 'became its own sandwich-man', with illustrations of book covers designed by George Auriol, Chéret, Willette, Steinlen and others.

A British monthly periodical called *The Poster* began publishing in June 1898, and the reproductions in its pages, in colour and monochrome, for five consecutive volumes maintain a startling standard of excellence. Here are, of course, Jules Chéret, Adolphe Mucha, Adolphe Willette and Eugène Grasset (among others) from France, Will Bradley from America, the Beggarstaffs, Dudley Hardy, John Hassall and Aubrey Beardsley from England, but in addition a flood of other designs of great distinction from many artists whose names are now less familiar than they deserve. *The Poster* occasionally devoted a page to 'Book Covers'; in another book, *Posters in Miniature,* New York & London, 1896, there are many magazine covers illustrated (e.g. *Harper's, The Inland Printer, The Century, La Revue Blanche, The Echo, The Chap Book, Lippincott's, Scribner's, The Bookman*), mostly of brilliant design quality, and some paper book covers, although none

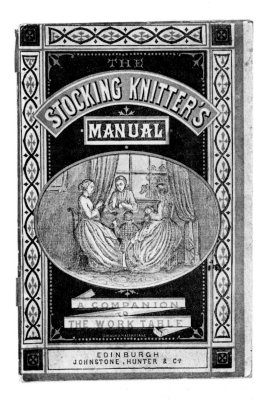

The Stocking Knitter's Manual
Edinburgh, Johnstone, Hunter & Co., 1878
165 × 112 mm

Paper on boards lithographed by Schenck & MacFarlane in red and blue.
Collection R. de Beaumont

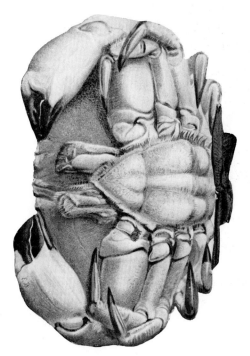

Seaside Memories
Nister, n.d. [1890s]
Back view of the ingenious shaped book shown on p.97. Note the binding ribbon at the back.
Collection R. de Beaumont

The Children's Shakespeare
E. Nesbit
Raphael Tuck, n.d. [1890s]
246 × 188 mm

Paper on boards, printed by chromolithography, red cloth spine.
Collection the late Percival Hinton

The Square Book of Animals
William Nicholson
W. Heinemann, 1900
177 × 175 mm

Paper printed in brown, yellow and
black.
*Reproduced from the facsimile edition
published by Scolar Press Ltd, 1979*

of the illustrations are captioned. New ideas in the design of publishers'
bindings were well illustrated in the winter number of *The Studio,*
1899-1900, *Modern Bookbindings and their Designers,* although most of
the work was on cloth: irritatingly, in that work, the material on which
the design was executed is usually ignored in the captions. In Brander
Matthews' *Bookbindings, Old and New,* 1896, (published in Gleeson
White's excellent Ex-libris series), a special section is devoted to 'Books
in Paper Covers', which the author points out were being neglected
by collectors: 'so far as I know, not any book-lover is now gathering
the books of all sorts which go forth to swift oblivion guarded against
hard usage only by a wrapper of paper.'

There were many designers who specialized in book cover design,
for example Gleeson White, Granville Fell, A. R. Turbayne, and
Talwin Morris; but covers were also being designed by artists of much
greater stature, such as Lucien Pissarro, Charles Ricketts, Laurence
Housman, Aubrey Beardsley and William Nicholson in Britain, Will
Bradley, E. A. Abbey and Howard Pyle in the U.S.A., and, in France,
Bonnard, Alexandre Steinlen, and Toulouse-Lautrec.

A booklet published in 1972 by Harvard College Library, *Toulouse-
Lautrec Book Covers and Brochures,* lists and illustrates no less than 24
items, the last being *The Motograph Moving Picture Book* published by
Bliss, Sands & Co. in London in 1898, with a lovely cover drawing
in colour by Toulouse-Lautrec, and inside the front cover 'a striated
plastic transparency may be removed and slid vertically over the
illustrations giving the illusion of a moving picture with changing
colors'. Peter Wick in his introduction to the catalogue writes 'one
soon becomes aware of a whole series of *livres de poches* and paper-
backs. . . . Even the great university libraries have neglected them.'
He also points out that some posters became book covers, and some
book covers became posters.

Paper was, and still is, accepted in France as a normal material for
the covers of new books, both in small, cheap, and large, expensive,
formats. In England, cloth was always the norm: nearly all William
Nicholson's dashing designs for Heinemann's book covers were
blocked in colours on cloth.

In Britain, at the turn of the century, there was a fashion for binding
books in white or light-coloured cloths, on which were blocked
designs in colours and gold which would have been more natural (if
less durable) on paper: an example is Ford M. Hueffer's *Ford Madox
Brown,* a charming design by W. H. Cowlishaw illustrated as frontispiece to the *Studio* winter number already mentioned. Later, in the
early years of the twentieth century, there seems to have been an
increased use of paper for bindings in Britain, for example by the
Edinburgh publisher T. N. Foulis, who produced a range of small
books in a variety of delightful paper covers, and who commissioned
the characteristic lettering used on his spines from the French designer
George Auriol. At this time also, many gift books for children and
adults were produced with full colour illustrations pasted onto cloth
covers.

The use of paper for publishers' bookbindings, not as a cheap sub-
stitute but as a positive element in the design, remained rare, but examples are all the more pleasing when they occur. If a design totally
obliterates the surface on which it is printed (as would a four-colour
half-tone) then the only quality demanded of that surface is that it
accepts the ink used; but paper deserves better than that. Although
the variety of papers, both hand-made and machine-made, now available for commercial use is less than in the nineteenth century, it remains an appropriate and indeed serviceable material for bookbindings
and an exciting challenge for designers.

Mr Tollet's Calendar
Manuscript 2525 in Pepys Library,
Cambridge, n.d. [*c.*1698]
350 × 280 mm

Bound in boards covered in two
different metallic varnish papers.
Described by Dr Mirjam Foot in *The
Book Collector*, Spring 1981, pp.74–5.
*By permission of the Master and Fellows
of Magdalene College, Cambridge*

Pine's *Horace*, 2 volumes
1733 (2nd issue)
246 × 150 mm

The paper is printed with an overall repeating pattern, engraved on wood, which is basically floral (like a William Morris design), apparently printed in olive green on green paper, and embossed, with random blobs of orange, purple and green added (by poupée?). The paper is pasted on boards, with the text paper used as end papers; the book titles, e.g. 'Horatii Opera Tom 1' hand-lettered on the spine in ink. Is this a 'publisher's binding'? The publisher may have caused a few sets to be bound thus. Such patterned papers (probably manufactured on the continent) at that period had domestic uses (e.g. lining drawers) as well as for book end papers and bindings.
Private Collection

A New History of England etc.
Printed for T. Carnan, 1785
104 × 68 mm

Brown or buff paper on boards, with woodcuts printed inside a typographical border in red, on front and back. See *Osborne*, vol. 2, p.789. This work was first published in 1759 by John Newbery. It is illustrated with woodcuts and the price of sixpence is printed on the title-page.
Collection R. de Beaumont

The Infant's Library
Printed and sold by John Marshall, London, n.d. [*c.*1800]
60 × 46 mm

Coloured paper on boards, with cut-out printed labels pasted down on front and back. The inside pages consist of extremely crudely printed text (from type) and illustrations (from wood and copper). There were 16 volumes. See *Osborne*, vol. 2, p.899 and illustration of model bookcase in Harvey Darton, *Children's Books in England*, 3rd edn, p.138.
Private Collection

The 103rd Psalm
Printed in Bristol by John Wright, n.d.
28 × 24 mm

Blue paper on card, printed in gold.
Private Collection

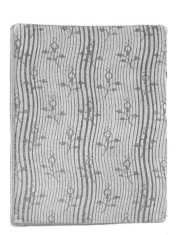

Hoyle's Games
Printed for R. Baldwin, etc., 1803
124 × 85 mm

Yellow unprinted paper covers, a.e.g., in slipcase of pink card, printed on all surfaces in black. This guide to popular card games may have been published in a slip-case to make it look similar to a pack of cards. The text is elegantly printed by C. Whittingham, Dean Street, Fetter Lane.
Collection John Porter

The Song of Moses
Wright & Albright, Avon St, Bristol, n.d. [1840]
60 × 50 mm

White card printed from wood in red and green.
Private Collection

Peter's Sermon on the Day of Pentecost
Wright & Albright, Avon St, Bristol, n.d. [1840]
60 × 52 mm

White card printed from wood in red and blue.
Private Collection

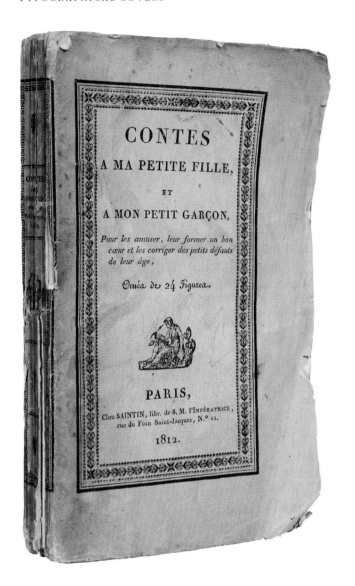

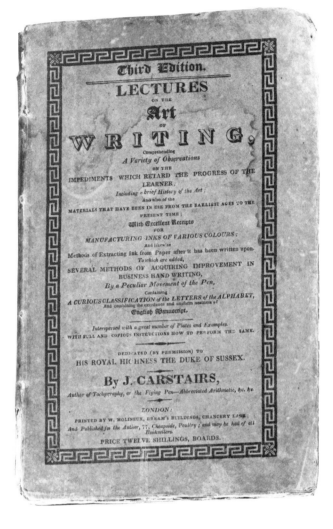

Contes à ma petite fille et à mon petit garçon etc.
Madame de Renneville
Paris, Chez Saintin, Libraire de
S.M. L'Impératrice, 1812
(deuxième édition)
180 × 110 mm

Buff paper printed from type on upper, spine and lower cover. Typographic design of upper cover is different from title-page, making this a true publisher's binding designed for display.
Title is also printed on spine.
Cf. Stendhal's *Armance*, 3v., Paris, 1827, repr. in *The Houghton Library 1942–1982*, Harvard College Library, 1982.
Massey College, Toronto, PB61

Lectures on the Art of Writing
J. Carstairs
London, printed by W. Molineux
and published for the Author, 1816
(3rd edition)
About 190 × 120 mm

Grey paper on boards.
A typographic cover design for display.
Collection B. L. Wolpe

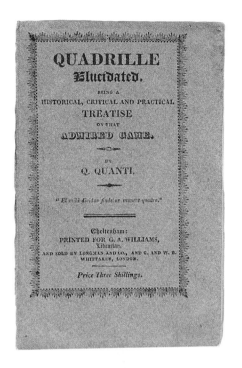

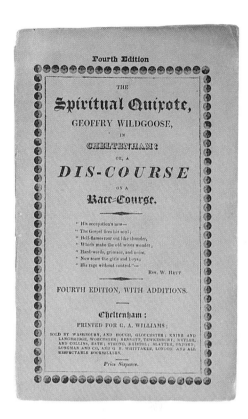

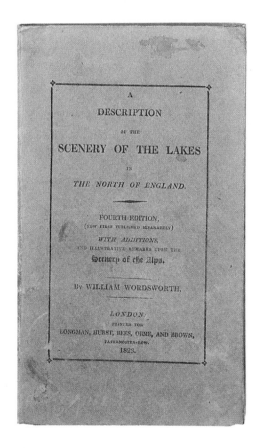

The Life and Exploits of Theodore Cyphon, or the Benevolent Jew: a Novel
George Walker
London: printed and sold by
S. Fisher, 1826
146 × 76 mm

Quadrille Elucidated
Q. Quanti
Cheltenham: printed for G. A. Williams, Librarian, and sold by Longman & Co., and G. and W. B. Whittaker, London, 1822
153 × 99 mm

Grey paper, printed from type in black on upper cover only. The title-page is similar to the cover, without the typographical border. Printed by Bennett, Tewkesbury.
Private Collection

The Spiritual Quixote etc.
J. Hawkins
Cheltenham, printed for G. A. Williams, 1827 (4th edition)
176 × 109 mm

Buff paper printed from type in black on upper cover only. The title page is similar to the cover, without the typographical border. Printed by J. J. Hadley, Cheltenham.
Private Collection

A Description of the Scenery of the Lakes etc.
William Wordsworth
Longman, 1823
186 × 110 mm

Pink paper on boards, printed in black from type on front, spine and back. The first separate publication of this work. The title is printed on the spine, reading upwards, and the type on the cover repeats the title-page, inside a plain border. Printed by A. & R. Spottiswoode.
Collection John Porter

Buff paper on boards, printed from type on front, spine and back. Sold with 7 engravings (etchings by W. Hopwood) at 3s.6d; the (six in this copy) etchings are dated at weekly intervals from 24 April to 29 May, 1824. All novels advertised on the front and back, which include *The Mysteries of Udolpho* and four other novels by Mrs Ann Radcliffe, were published in sixpenny parts.
Private Collection

A New Book of Games and Forfeits etc.
Dean & Munday, n.d. (coloured
frontispiece dated 1833)
178 × 110 mm

Yellow pages pasted on card, printed
in black. Dean & Munday were
pioneers of Toy Books, and although
this particular item was for adults, the
back cover lists 18 titles headed
'Nursery Tales and Toy Books, one
shilling each', the same price as this
book.
Private Collection

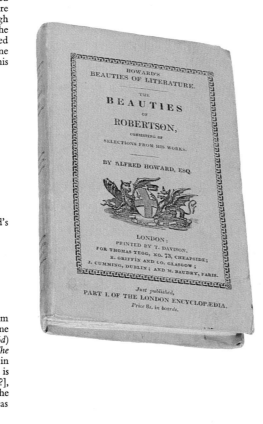

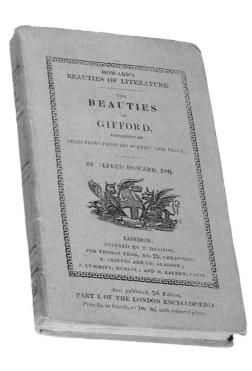

The Beauties of Robertson
The Beauties of Gifford
Vols. XXXI and XXXV in Howard's
'Beauties of Literature', edited by
Alfred Howard, printed by T.
Davison, Whitefriars, for Thomas
Tegg, London, R. Griffin, Glasgow
and J. Cumming, Dublin, n.d.
('[1834?]' in B.M. Catalogue)
148 × 92 mm

Buff paper on boards, printed from
type and woodblocks on front, spine
and back. The titles and price (2s.6d)
are printed on the spines. Vol. 1, *The
Beauties of Addison*, Part 1, bound in
the same style of paper on boards, is
dated by the British Museum [1829?],
since it carries a reference to the
London Encyclopaedia which was
published in 1829.
Private Collection

*Cornelia, Taschenbuch für Deutsche
Frauen*
Heidelberg, Joseph Engelmann
3rd year, 1818
127 × 97 mm

Buff paper on boards printed from
etched plates in black on front, spine
and back, all edges gilt [a.e.g.]. This
was a ladies' annual, edited by Aloys
Schreiber, containing stories, poems,
etched illustrations and a folding
plate of music. The illustrations on
the cover represent (according to the
editor's foreword) the ancient German Goddesses Wara (marriage and
fidelity) and Geffiona (youth and
innocence). Their names are spelled
below in runic characters which are,
according to Diringer, 'The "national" writing of the Teutons, especially
of the North Germanic peoples'.
Collection Michael Twyman

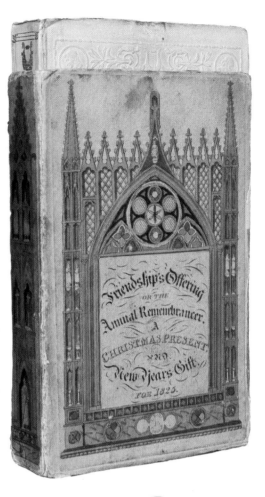

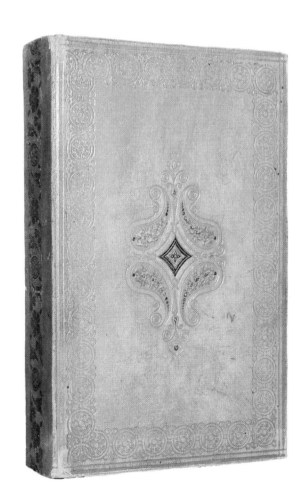

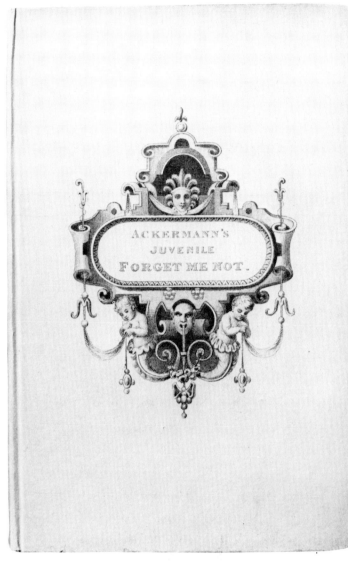

◁

Friendship's Offering, or, The Annual Remembrancer . . . For 1825
Lupton Relfe, [1824]
144 × 92 mm

Pink paper on boards, blind-embossed in classical pattern on upper and lower cover, blocked in gold on spine, with title, a.e.g. Enclosed in open-ended carton with hand-coloured etched plate pasted on upper, with design in similar gothic style pasted down on both narrow sides. A highly elaborate and attractive 'package' for a Christmas gift book. The first title-page is etched, hand-coloured in gold and colours, different from the 'jacket' design shown here. Sold at 12s. (ECB).
Massey College, Toronto, PB63

◁

The Amulet
W. Baynes & Son, and Wightman & Cramp, 1828 [1827]
142 × 89 mm (carton 147 × 92 mm)

Carton, purple paper on card, with printed designs pasted down on all sides (five labels in all). See also p.10. *The Amulet* itself was bound in purple watered silk and is illustrated in VPBCL, p.20. Sold at 12s. (ECB).
Massey College, Toronto, PB68

◁

Forget Me Not: A Christmas and New Year's Present for MDCCCXXVII
Edited by Frederic Shoberl
R. Ackermann, [1826]
142 × 87 mm

Emerald green paper on boards with designs printed (by lithography?) on upper, lower and spine, a.e.g. Enclosed in buff paper open-ended carton (not shown), with same designs as on book, on emerald paper, pasted down on upper and lower. Sold at 12s. (ECB).
Massey College, Toronto, PB65

◁

Forget Me Not etc., for MDCCCXXX
Edited by Frederic Shoberl
R. Ackermann, [1829]
148 × 94 mm
This book was bound in crimson watered silk, blocked in gold, and is illustrated in VPBCL, p.20. Shown here is the open-ended carton, pink paper with design printed in red, green, and blue, on upper and lower, blocked in gold on all sides. Another highly attractive Christmas 'package'.
Massey College, Toronto, PB64

Juvenile Forget Me Not
Edited by Frederic Shoberl
R. Ackermann, 1831 [1830]
145 × 95 mm

Cream paper on boards printed in black on upper and lower. No concession is made to children in this sophisticated design, but perhaps Ackermann considered it would be bought chiefly by adults.
Collection R. de Beaumont

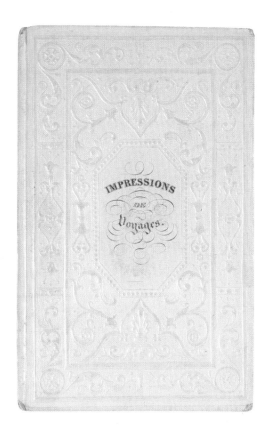

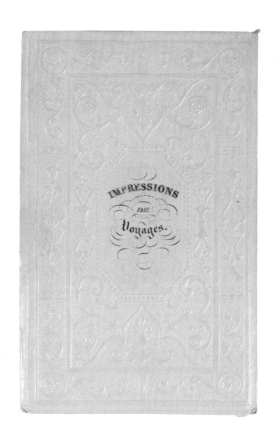

Impressions de Voyages, Promenades Pittoresques en France
(La Grande Chartreuse, Les Roches de Baume, Notre-Dame de Mont-Thabor)
Paris, Marcilly, n.d. [*c*.1835]
153 × 97 mm

Ivory glazed paper on boards with decorative design blind-stamped on upper, short title lithographed in black.

Printed by Firmin Didot Frères with one hand-coloured illustration ('Pont sur le Guyer').
Massey College, Toronto, PB82

Impressions de Voyages etc. (Une Fête à Alger, Le Chateau de Roche-Chinard, Niederbroun)
Paris, Marcilly, n.d. [*c*.1835]

As PB82, but blue glazed paper. One hand-coloured illustration ('Une Fête à Alger').
Gumuchian, *Livres de l'Enfance*, Nos 3128–3130.
Massey College, Toronto, PB81

The Squib Annual of Poetry, Politics, and Personalities, for MDCCCXXXVI
Illustrated by R. Seymour
Chapman & Hall, 1836 [1835]
154 × 99 mm

Cream-yellow paper on boards printed in black with pictorial designs by Seymour on upper, spine, and lower.
Price 5s.
Massey College, Toronto, PB79

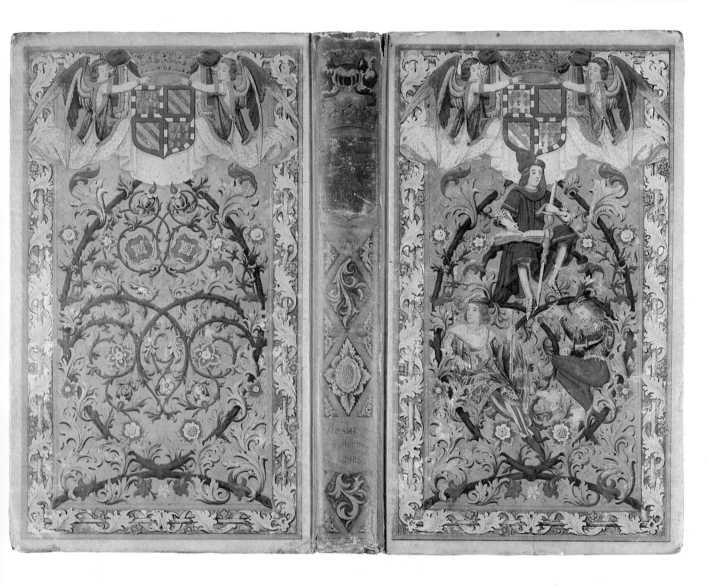

Les Ducs de Bourgogne etc.
F. Valentin
Tours, Mame et cie, 1842
220 × 135 mm

Paper on boards printed in rich
chromolithography on upper, spine
and lower. The firm of Mame became one of the biggest printers and
publishers in France, and specialized
in decorative paper bindings: see
pp.46–8.
Collection R. de Beaumont

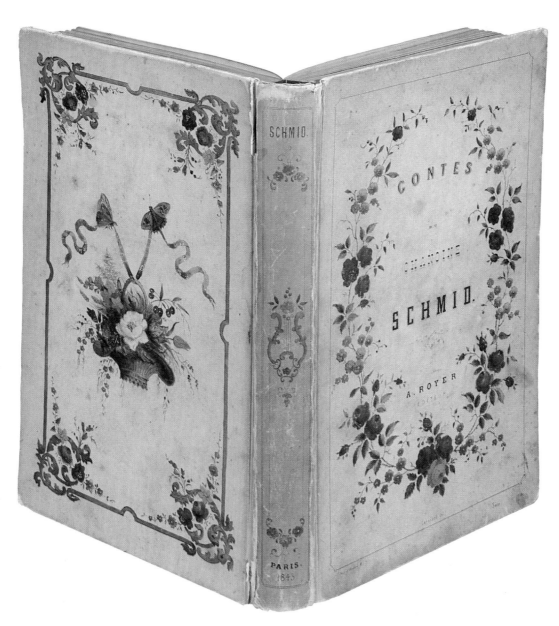

Contes du Chanoine Schmid
Transl. A. Cerfberr de Medelsheim
Paris, A. Royer, 1843
260 × 164 mm

White or cream paper on boards
designed by Cagniard, printed lithographically on upper, spine and lower
by Aubert, richly hand-coloured.
The book contains illustrations by
Gavarni: see Gumuchian, item 5139.
Massey College, Toronto, PB93

Lays of the Palace
The Poetry by Charles James Jefferys,
the music by Sidney Nelson
Illustrated by John Brandard
Monro & May, 1841
351 × 260 mm

White glazed paper on boards,
printed in gold on upper only, green
leather spine without lettering. The
book is dedicated by the publishers to
Prince Albert. The cover design
shows the Collar and George of the
Garter, with the Prince's arms at the
top, and inside that, the title, and,
within that again, the star of the
Garter. There was a fashion in the
1840s and 1850s for big 'drawing
room' books in white covers printed
simply in gold; very few have survived in reproducible condition. Sold
at 12s.6d (ECB).
Massey College, Toronto, PB74

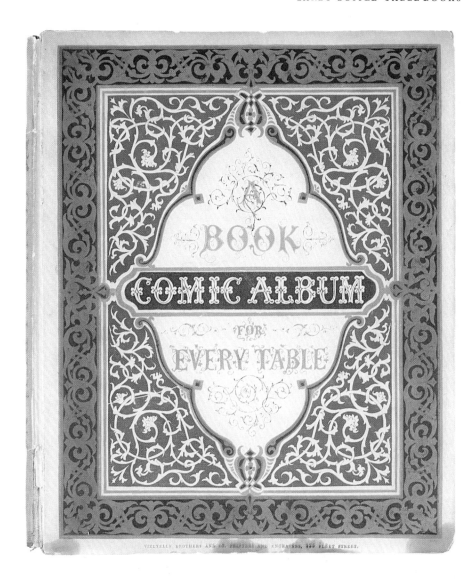

The Comic Album: A Book for Every Table
W. S. Orr, 1843
265 × 220 mm

White paper on boards printed by Vizetelly Bros in blue, red and gold. Vizetelly printed *Ancient Spanish Ballads* in 1841 and 1842, with designs by Owen Jones which may have influenced this cover. Each section of the book is printed on different coloured paper.
Massey College, Toronto, PB88

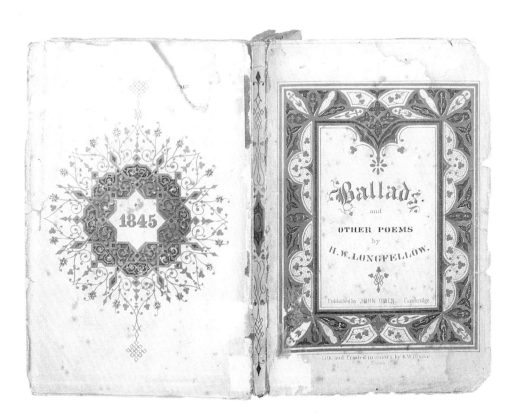

Ballads and other Poems
H. W. Longfellow
John Owen, Cambridge (Mass.), 1845
180 × 120 mm

Paper chromolithographed in blue, red and gold by E. W. Bouvé, Boston. The first American chromolithograph (according to P. C. Marzio, *The Democratic Art*, 1980) was printed in Boston in 1840 by William Sharp, a Londoner who later had a partnership in Boston with E. W. Bouvé.
Collection R. de Beaumont

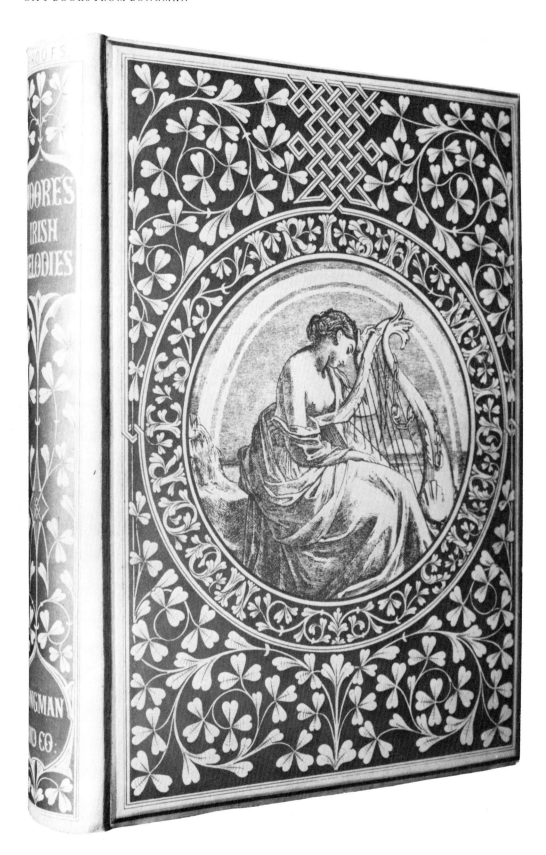

Moore's Irish Melodies
Illustrated by Daniel Maclise
Longman, 1846
278 × 194 mm

Cream paper on bevelled boards, printed in green and gold on upper, spine and lower. Note the skilful introduction of the title into the circle round the illustration. One of the finest covers of the early Victorian period, probably designed by Owen Jones. The back is shown on p.13.
Collection R. de Beaumont

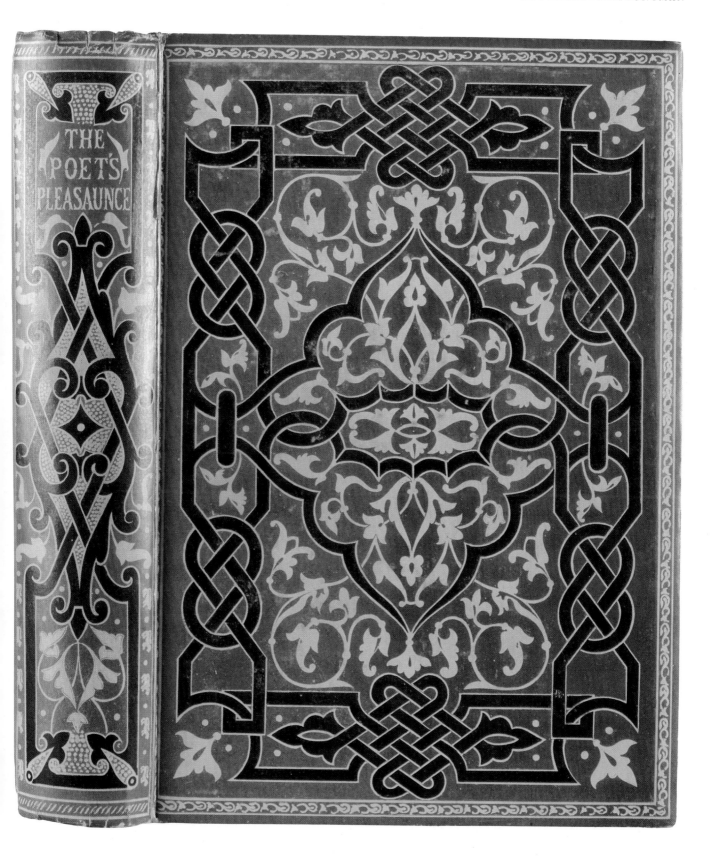

The Poets' Pleasaunce
Eden Warwick
Illustrated by H. Noel Humphreys
Longman, 1847
227 × 157 mm

Grey-green paper on bevelled boards, printed in yellow and black on upper, spine and lower. The design, repeated on upper and lower, is a version of the 'Erasmus pattern' illustrated in Henry Shaw's *The Encyclopaedia of Ornament*, 1842, plate 6, 'taken from a copy of Erasmus on the New Testament, in the possession of Mr Pickering'. See p.11. Sold at 30s.; remaindered by Tegg in 1849 at 21s. (ECB). *Massey College, Toronto*, PB84.

A Booke of Christmas Carols, Illuminated from Ancient Manuscripts in the British Museum
Henry G. Bohn, n.d. [1845]
198 × 143 mm

White glazed paper on boards, printed in blue, yellow, green, purple and gold, and embossed. The embossing on this design (and its total irrelevance to the subject of the book) reminds one of the French romantic bindings of the same period shown on pp.46–8. A different design, printed in blue and gold only, is printed on the lower cover. This book was the concept of, and selected by, Joseph Cundall, whose name is on the title-page as publisher in some copies. It was drawn and lithographed by John Brandard, chromolithographed by M. & N. Hanhart, and the type was set and printed by Charles Whittingham.
Massey College, Toronto, JC54

The Works of Quintus Horatius Flaccus
With a life by H. H. Milman
John Murray, 1849
220 × 145 mm

Terracotta glazed paper on boards
printed in black by lithography. The
design is by Owen Jones, who provided 8 chromolithographed title-
pages and coloured and monochrome
decorations for the book – one of his
masterpieces of decoration.
Collection R. de Beaumont

The Art of Etching on Copper
Alfred Ashley
J. &. D. A. Darling, n.d. [1849]
222 × 278 mm

Glazed white paper on boards, red
cloth spine. A 'How to do it' book
published by a firm of London
printers, with a cover design in black,
blue, gold, and red which has no
visual connection at all with the subject of the book. It is in the illuminated style of Owen Jones, and was
probably drawn by him. Most sur-
prisingly, it was cut on wood and
printed by letterpress, rather than
drawn on stone and lithographed,
which would have seemed more
suitable for such a complicated design.
The lower cover carries an illuminated monogram of the author's
initials printed in the same colours.
Massey College, Toronto, J43

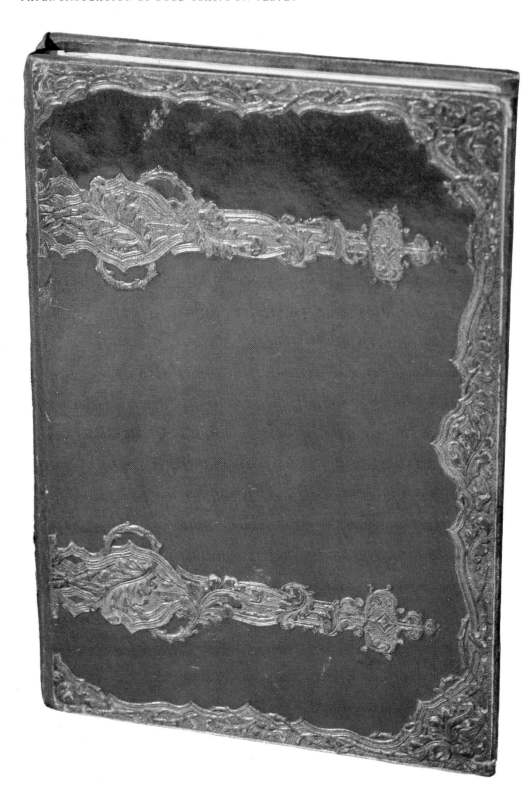

The Coins of England
Henry Noel Humphreys
William Smith, 1846
198 × 132 mm

Red paper blind embossed and printed in gold. This binding design, an ingenious and ambitious simulation in paper of gold clasps on red velvet, was continued on later editions, published by Longman, up to the sixth published by Bohn in 1849.
Massey College, Toronto, H3

Choice Examples of Art Workmanship etc.
Drawn and engraved under the superintendance of Philip de la Motte Cundall & Addey, and George Bell, 1851
288 × 185 mm

Paper on boards, printed from wood in yellow, red and black, with green and blue added (by stencil). Brass corner studs have been fitted to upper and lower covers to prevent the covers from being rubbed. The book has no text, but consists only of wood-engraved illustrations. These are mostly uncoloured in the 'smaller edition', which this copy is, but are all hand-coloured in the large paper copies. This cover design appears on the 'smaller edition' only; in the large paper edition, normally bound in leather by Hayday, it appears as the last illustration, and is captioned 'a morocco binding having sunk panels in which are embossed arabesques on a gold ground. Sixteenth century. The design from this book has been used on the binding of the smaller edition of the present work. S. Ram, Esq.'

The present location of the original book referred to, if it still exists, is unknown, but I am indebted to Mr H. M. Nixon for the following comment: 'The design is probably based on French bindings of the Grolier period but includes a centre-piece bearing the title, whose outline is purely oriental. The French tools of this Grolier period are themselves based on earlier oriental designs.'
Collection R. de Beaumont

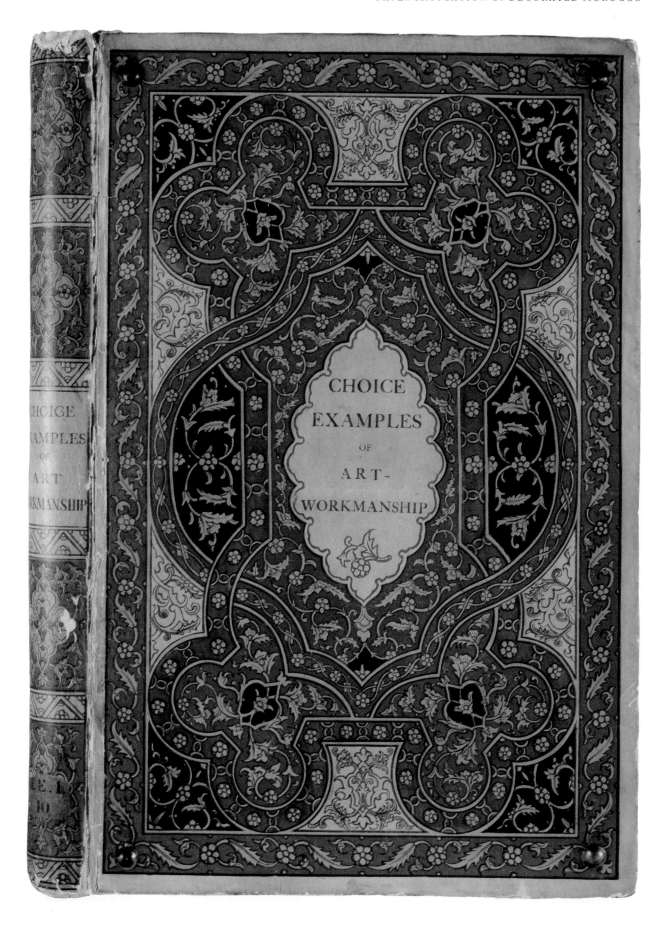

PAPER SIMULATION OF DECORATED MOROCCO

CHOICE EXAMPLES OF ART-WORKMANSHIP

PAPER SIMULATION OF DECORATED MOROCCO

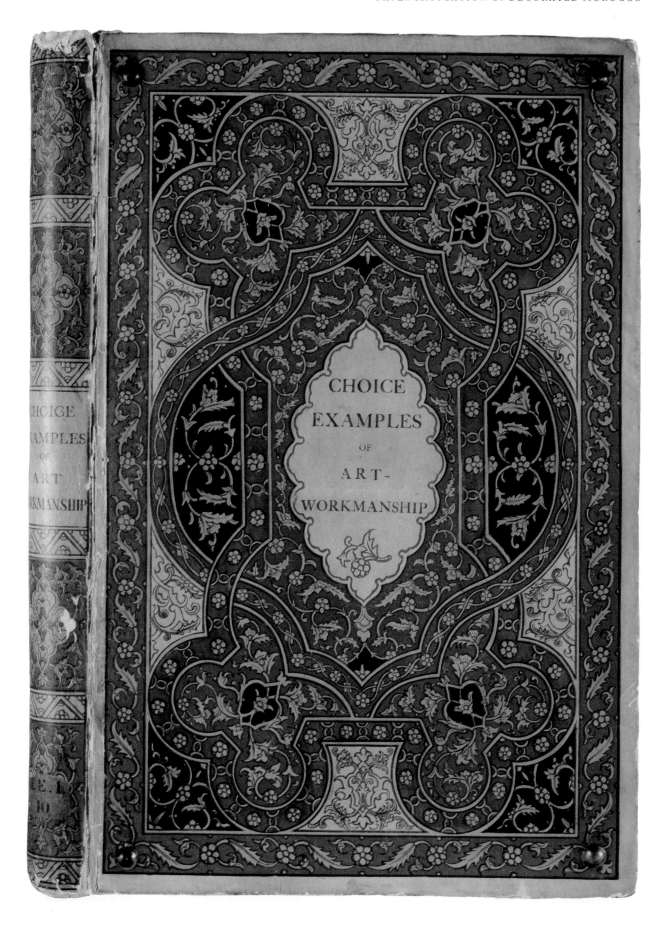

35

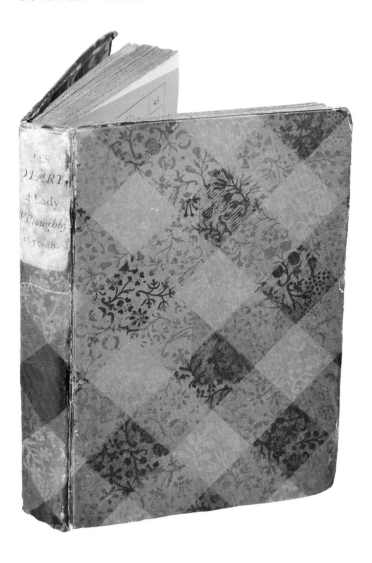

*So much of the Diary of Lady
Willoughby as relates to her Domestic
History etc.*
Longman, 1845
174 × 118 mm

Paper on boards, printed in blue,
green, red, yellow and gold, with
printed label on spine. This invented
diary and its sequels, written pseud-
onymously by Hannah Mary Rathbone, appeared in a number of different binding styles, including leather
by Hayday. The three 'Dutch'
patterned papers shown on this page
were presumably supposed to have
antiquarian associations (the text is
set in the Civil War period), as was
the allusive Chiswick Press typography of the text. All three were
bound by Remnant & Edmonds.
Sold at 8s. (ECB).
Massey College, Toronto, PB47

*So much of the Diary of Lady
Willoughby etc.*
Longman, 1846 (4th edition)
174 × 118 mm

Emerald green paper on boards,
printed with pattern in gold, with
printed label on spine. The same
design is also found on copies of this
book, printed in gold on red paper;
and in black, with colours overprinted, on *Some Further Portions* etc.,
below, right.
Collection R. de Beaumont

*Some Further Portions of the Diary of
Lady Willoughby etc.*
Longman, 1848
174 × 118 mm

Paper on boards, printed with pattern
in black, and then overprinted in red,
mauve, yellow, green, blue and red
(split-duct?) and embossed with fine
ribbing, with printed label on spine.
Collection Fianach Lawry

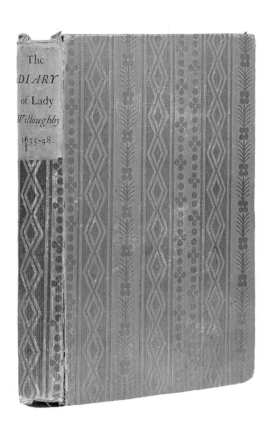

Chambers's Miscellany of Useful and Entertaining Tracts, Vol X
Edinburgh, W. & R. Chambers, 1846
188 × 115 mm

White paper on boards, printed from type and wood in red, blue and ochre. The same design is printed on upper and lower. This popular series sold at 1s. per volume.
Private Collection

Chambers's Papers for the People, Vol. IV
Edinburgh, W. & R. Chambers, 1850
206 × 130 mm

Yellow glazed paper printed from wood in red and green. This series 'mainly addressed to that numerous class whose minds have been educated by the improved schooling, and the popular lectures and publications, of the last twenty years' was published in weekly numbers at 1½d, in monthly parts at 7d, and in 'Volumes, every two months, in fancy-coloured boards, at 1s.6d.' Cf. the use of yellow glazed paper by Simms & McIntyre for their Parlour Library from 1847 (see VBD, p.220 and pl. xv) and Edmund Evans' 'yellow-backs' with pictorial designs from c.1853.
Massey College, Toronto, PB89

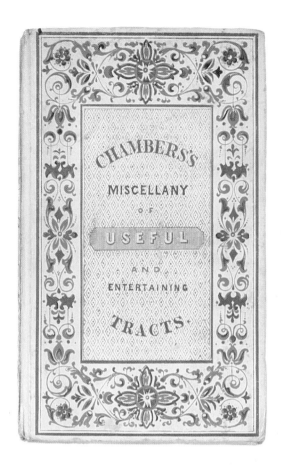

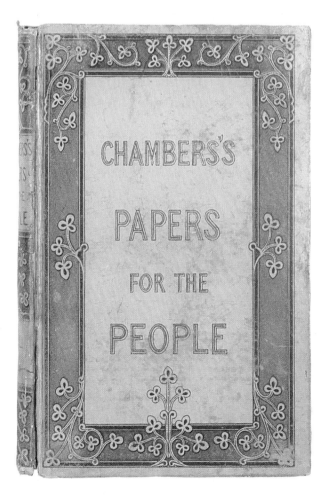

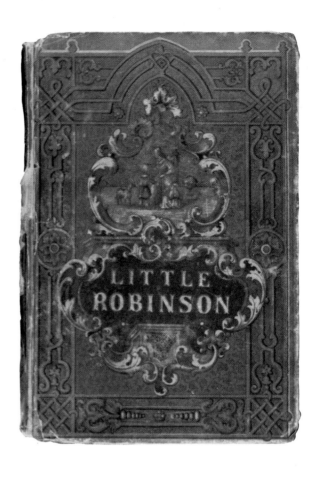

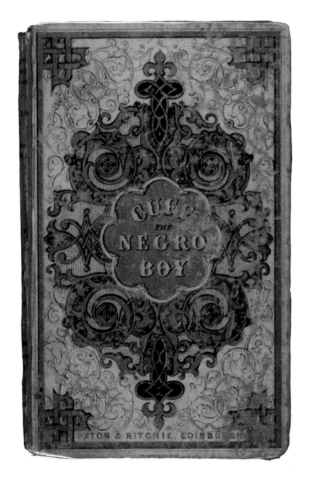

The Mother's Primer: A little Child's first Steps in many ways
Mrs Felix Summerly (pseudonym of the wife of Henry Cole)
Longman, 1844
166 × 124 mm

Paper, printed from wood in red, yellow and blue. Printed by the Chiswick Press.
This little book is a remarkably advanced introduction to reading and writing for children. It was reproduced in facsimile for the Friends of the Osborne and Lilian H. Smith Collections of Early Children's Books in Toronto Public Library, in 1970 (from a copy of which this reproduction has been made). In her introduction, Miss Judith St John writes: '*The Mother's Primer* was Lady Cole's only known contribution to the Home Treasury Series . . . it seems highly probable that it was Lady Cole who brought to her busy husband's attention the need for publishing old nursery tales and legends and that, as his 'best adviser', she unobtrusively assisted him in the selection and the editing of the texts.'

The Young Lady's Monitor, and Married Woman's Friend
Mrs Maxwell
Edinburgh, N. Bowack, 1845
(5th edition)
105 × 67 mm

Paper, lithographed in gold, red, green, blue and black. The title-page has a different elaborate design lithographed in colours.
Private Collection

Poetical Remembrances of Lynmouth
Maia
Barnstaple: printed and sold by W. Avery, 1845
137 × 105 mm

White glazed paper on boards, lithographed in black and hand-coloured, grey cloth spine. An ambitious and charming example of provincial printing, probably in a very small edition.
Private Collection

The Poetry of Flowers etc.
by the Editor of the 'Language of Flowers'
James Williams, 1845
142 × 88 mm

Glazed paper, lithographed in two shades of gold, red, yellow, blue and black, by MacLure & Macdonald, Glasgow, a.e.g.
Private Collection

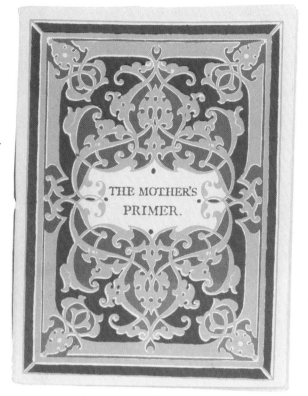

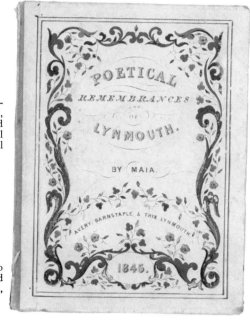

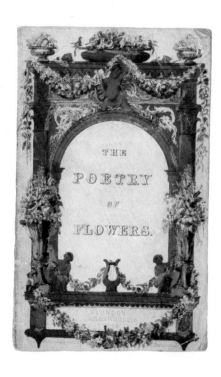

◁

Grandmamma's Pockets
Mrs S. C. Hall
(Chambers's Library for Young People)
Edinburgh, W. & R. Chambers, 1849
149 × 102 mm

Emerald green paper on boards, lithographed in dark blue and gold.
Massey College, Toronto, PB39

◁

The Little Robinson
(Chambers's Library for Young People)
Edinburgh, W. & R. Chambers, 1848
148 × 100 mm

Paper on boards, lithographed in red, reddish-brown, white, blue and gold by F. R. Schenck.
Massey College, Toronto, PB37

◁

Cuff, the Negro Boy
Rev. R. Menzies
Edinburgh, Paton & Ritchie, 1848
148 × 92 mm

Pink paper on boards, printed by lithography in blue and black.
Massey College, Toronto, PB36

◁

Historic Gleanings
(Holmes' Popular Library)
Thomas Holmes, n.d. [c.1851]
146 × 95 mm

Mauve paper lithographed in black and gold by Hullmandel. Four highly sophisticated and attractive designs on cheap children's series.
Massey College, Toronto, PB38

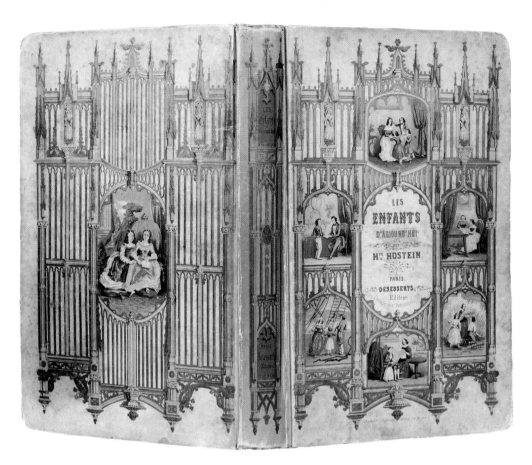

Les Enfants d' Aujourd' hui
Hippolyte Hostein
Paris, A. Desesserts, n.d. [1844 in
B.M. catalogue]
246 × 154 mm

Paper on boards, chromolithographed
by Engelmann & Graf on upper,
spine, and lower. A magnificently
'packaged' children's book, illustrated
inside with hand-coloured litho-
graphs and wood-engravings.
Massey College, Toronto, PB70

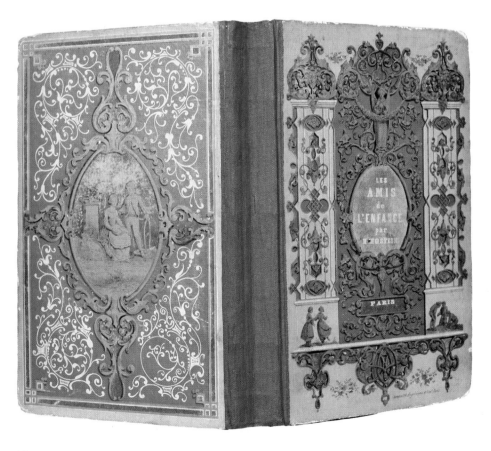

Les Amis de l'Enfance
Hippolyte Hostein
Paris, Louis Janet, n.d. [1848 in
B.M. catalogue]
228 × 147 mm

Paper on boards, chromolithographed
by Engelmann & Graf on upper,
spine and lower (this copy re-backed
in dark-blue cloth). Another beautifully produced and illustrated children's book from France. Again,
highly sophisticated in design.
Massey College, Toronto, PB71

Les Emotions d'un jeune Mousse
M. Castillon
(Grande Bibliothèque Illustrée)
Paris, A. Courcier, n.d. [1862, B.N.]
315 × 220 mm

Paper on boards with pictorial chromolithographed design (this copy re-backed in dark-red cloth). A splendid cover more obviously designed for children.
Massey College, Toronto, PB73

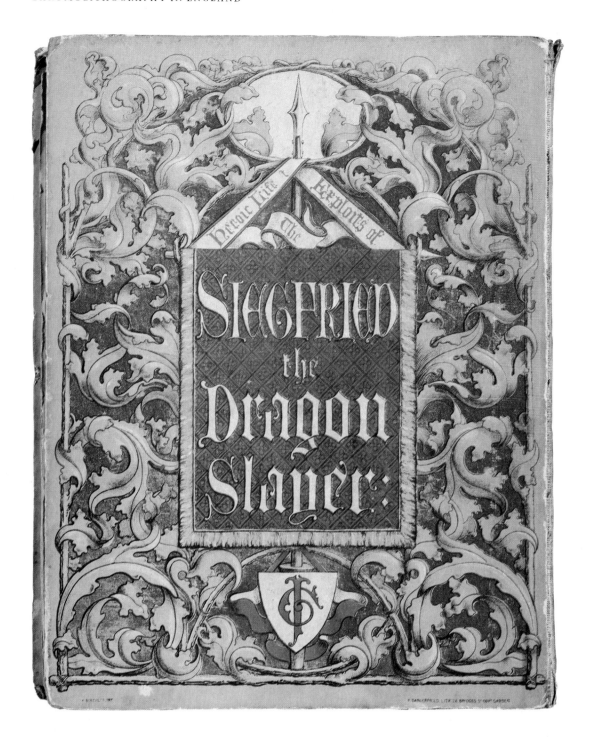

*The Heroic Life and Exploits of Siegfried
the Dragon Slayer*
Wilhelm Kaulbach
Joseph Cundall & David Bogue, 1848
227 × 175 mm

Paper on boards chromolithographed
in blue, red, ochre and black, signed
at foot of lower cover, 'R. BUR-
CHETT INV' and 'F. DANGER-
FIELD LITH: 26, BRYDGES St
COVt GARDEN'. Burchett also
designed the paper cover of Cundall's
The Playmate (ill. in colour in *Joseph
Cundall* 1976, p.24) using motifs very
similar to those used in *Nursery
Rhymes* opposite. Sold at 7s.6d, or
coloured 12s. (ECB). This copy is
uncoloured.
Massey College, Toronto, JC129

Nursery Rhymes, with the tunes to which they are still sung in the Nurseries of England etc.
Collected and edited by Edward F. Rimbault
Cramer, Beale & Co. n.d. [1849: cf. *Osborne*, vol 2, p.687]
213 × 166 mm

Paper on boards, chromolithographed with different designs on upper and lower, green cloth spine, a.e.g. These designs, unsigned, might have been drawn by R. Burchett, the designer of *Siegfried the Dragon Slayer* opposite. Sold at 6s. (ECB). Upper cover, *above*; lower cover, *left*.
Massey College, Toronto, PB83

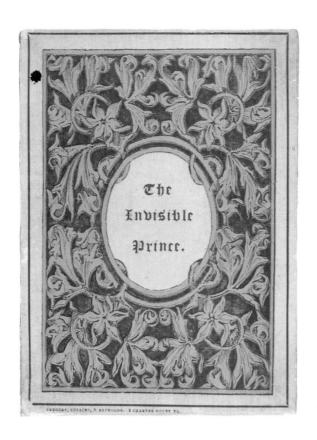

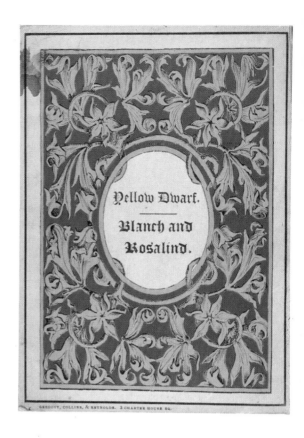

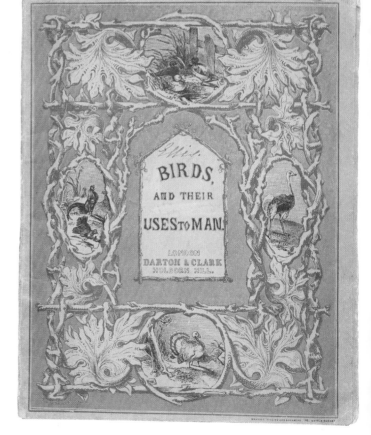

The Invisible Prince
James Burns, n.d. [1848]
165 × 123 mm

Paper, printed from wood in brown, green and blue by Gregory, Collins & Reynolds.
Massey College, Toronto, CR12

The Yellow Dwarf
James Burns, n.d. [1848]
165 × 122 mm (same blocks as preceding)

Paper, printed from wood in black, green and dark brown by Gregory, Collins & Reynolds.
Massey College, Toronto, CR11

The Young Ladies' Letter Writer
Mrs Alexander Walker
Darton & Co., n.d. [1848]
119 × 76 mm

Beige paper, with strapwork design printed in black, red and blue.
Massey College, Toronto, PB76

Birds, and their Uses to Man
Darton & Clark, n.d. [c.1846: Clark withdrew from the partnership in 1847; see *Osborne*, vol 1, p.472]
204 × 166 mm

Grey paper, printed in red, blue, gold

▷

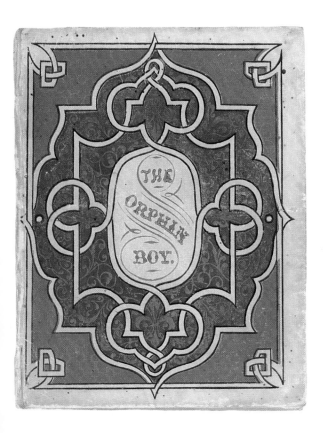

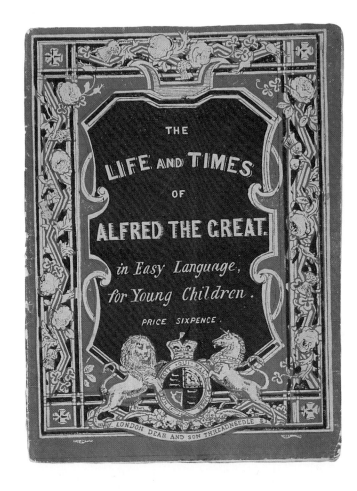

The Orphan Boy
Mary Elliot(t)
Darton & Clark, n.d. [1845]
142 × 110 mm

Paper on boards, printed from wood in black, red, blue and gold in same design on upper and lower, in blue and black on spine, a.e.g. This story has a pictorial title-page printed in colours and gold from wood (probably by Gregory, Collins & Reynolds) and four hand-coloured lithographed illustrations. Sold at *2s.6d* (ECB).
Massey College, Toronto, PB90

The Life and Times of Alfred the Great
M.J.C. (Julia Corner)
Thomas Dean, n.d. [1850: see *Osborne*, vol. 1, p.163]
166 × 124 mm

Card, lithographed in red-brown and blue. An illustrated booklet sold at *6d*.
Private Collection

A Book about Birds
The Religious Tract Society, n.d. (inscribed 1853)
185 × 138 mm

Pink paper with ripple grain on boards, lithographed in gold and blue. One of a series of children's books with colour plates by Kronheim.
Private Collection

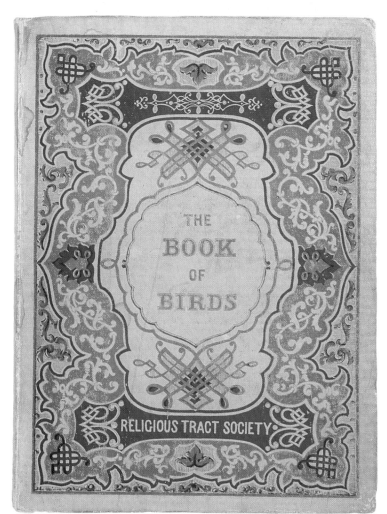

and black. Block on upper cover is signed 'R. A. HARRISON INV' and below the block is printed, in black from type, 'GREGORY, COLLINS AND REYNOLDS, 108 HATTON GARDEN'. Sold at *1s*.
Massey College, Toronto, CR24

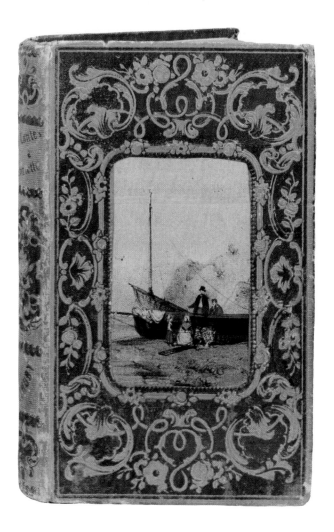

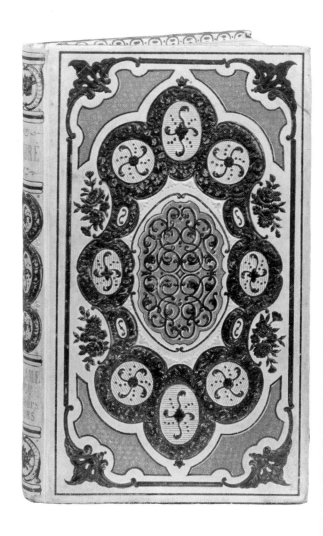

Contes à Henriette
Abel Dufresne
Paris, P.–C. Lehuby, 1843 (9e édition)
146 × 88 mm

Blue paper on boards, printed in gold
and embossed, with cut-out panel on
upper overlaid on hand-coloured
lithographic plate. The lower cover
is from the same plate as the upper,
with decorative central panel not cut
out.
Private Collection

André, ou Bonheur dans la Piété
Mme Césarie Farrenc
Tours, Mame et Cie, 1848
144 × 86 mm

White paper on boards, printed in
green and gold and embossed. The
upper and lower are the same.
Private Collection

Vie de M. De la Motte,
Évêque d'Amiens
l'Abbé Proyart
Paris et Limoges, Martial Ardant
Frères, 1845
179 × 105 mm

Dark blue grained and glazed paper
on boards, printed in gold and embossed.
Private Collection

Histoire des Chevaliers de Malte
l'Abbé de Vertot
Tours, Mame et Cie, 1855 (7e édition)
190 × 110 mm

White paper on boards, printed in
red, green and gold, and embossed,
with cut-out panel on upper overlaid
on chromolithographed plate. The
lower is the same as the upper, with
decorative panel not cut out.
Private Collection

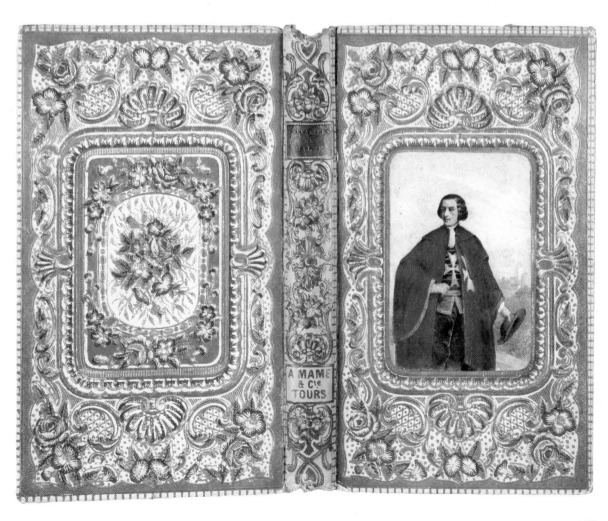

Les Incas etc.
Marmontel
Tours, Mame et Cie, 1855 (7e édition)
190 × 110 mm

White paper printed in pink, green
and gold, and embossed, with cut-out
panel on upper overlaid on chromolithographed plate. The lower is the
same as the upper, with decorative
central panel not cut out.
Private Collection

English Hexameter Translations etc.
John Murray, 1847
142 × 217 mm

Red paper on boards, lithographed in
black and gold. Upper, *above* and
lower, *below*. The design is characteristic of the work of Owen Jones.
Collection R. de Beaumont

Holy Bible
Edinburgh, 1843
143 × 89 mm

Black papier-mâché sides and spine, with leather hinge, spine lettered 'Holy Bible'. Printed by Sir D. Hunter Blair and R. M. S. Tyndall Bruce.
Collection Bernard Middleton

Holy Bible
George Eyre & William Spottiswoode, 1847
148 × 86 mm

Black papier-mâché. This front cover was also used on *The Book of Common Prayer*, Eyre & Spottiswoode, n.d., bound with *The Psalms*, printed by Brady & Tate, 1849.
Massey College, Toronto PB(L)27

Quarles' Emblems
1845
Brown papier-mâché covers cast from same mould as 1843 Bible on left. Same design on spine but now lettered 'Quarles' Emblems'.
Collection Eric Quayle

Holy Bible
G. E. Eyre & W. Spottiswoode, 1851
130 × 82 mm (page size)

Black papier-mâché. Upper cover is signed D. O. Smith, London.

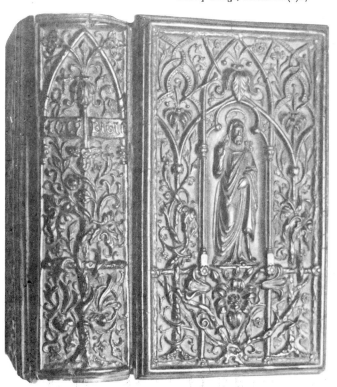

Parables of Our Lord
Illuminated by H. N. Humphreys
Longman, 1847
166 × 115 mm

Black papier-mâché.
Massey College, Toronto, H14

The Good Shunamite
Illuminated by Lewis Gruner
Longman, 1847
c. 162 × 112 mm

Black papier-mâché.
Massey College, Toronto, IB42

The Miracles of Our Lord
Illuminated by H. N. Humphreys
Longman, 1848
172 × 122 mm

Black papier-mâché.
Massey College, Toronto, H16

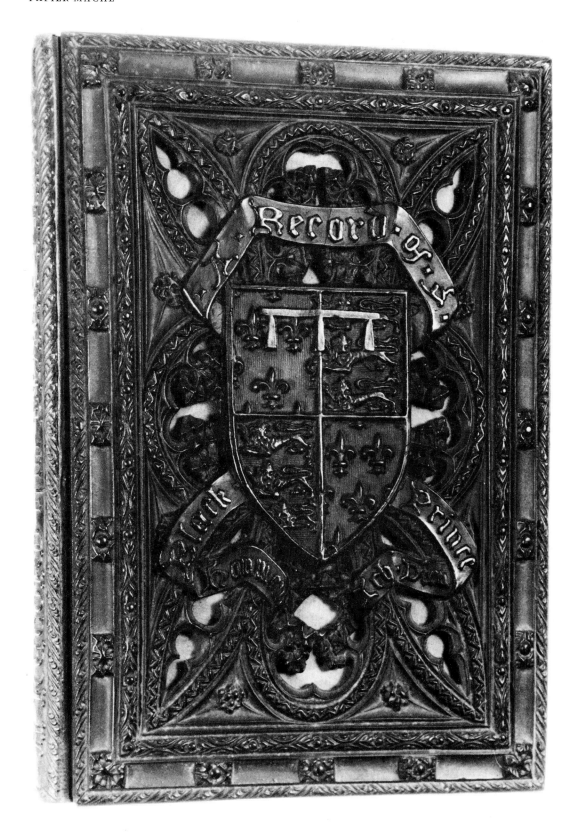

A Record of the Black Prince
Illuminated by H. N. Humphreys
Longman, 1849
195 × 134 mm

Black papier-mâché over crimson
paper.
Massey College, Toronto, H22

Many Thoughts of Many Minds
H. Southgate
Griffin, 1863
209 × 145 mm

Black papier-mâché, upper cover adapted from *A Record of the Black Prince*, with new border.
Private Collection

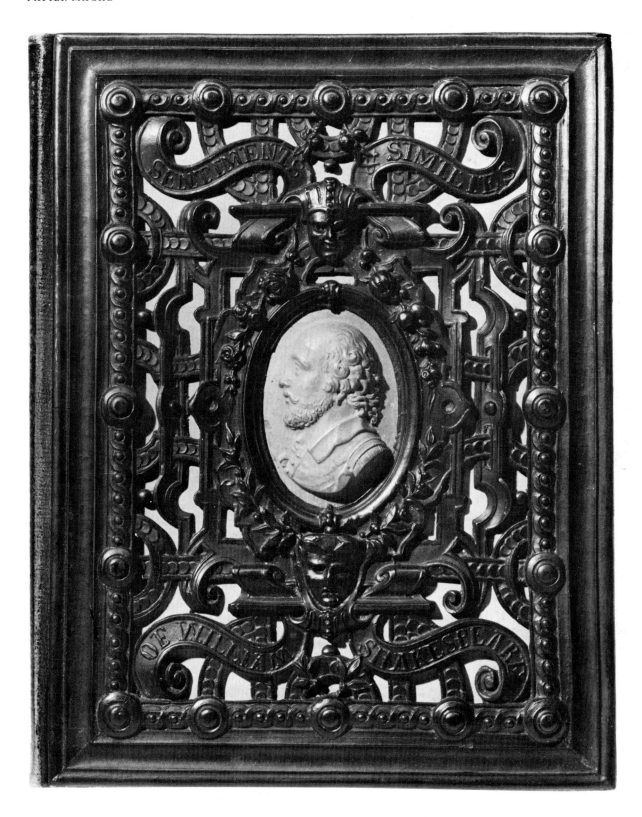

*Sentiments and Similes of William
Shakespeare*
H. N. Humphreys
Longman, 1857 (2nd edition)
198 × 149 mm

Black papier-mâché on crimson
paper, terracotta portrait medallion
of William Shakespeare on upper and
monogram of his initials on lower.
First edition (1851) identical but on
gold paper. Leather spine. Sold at
1 guinea (ECB).
Massey College, Toronto, H27

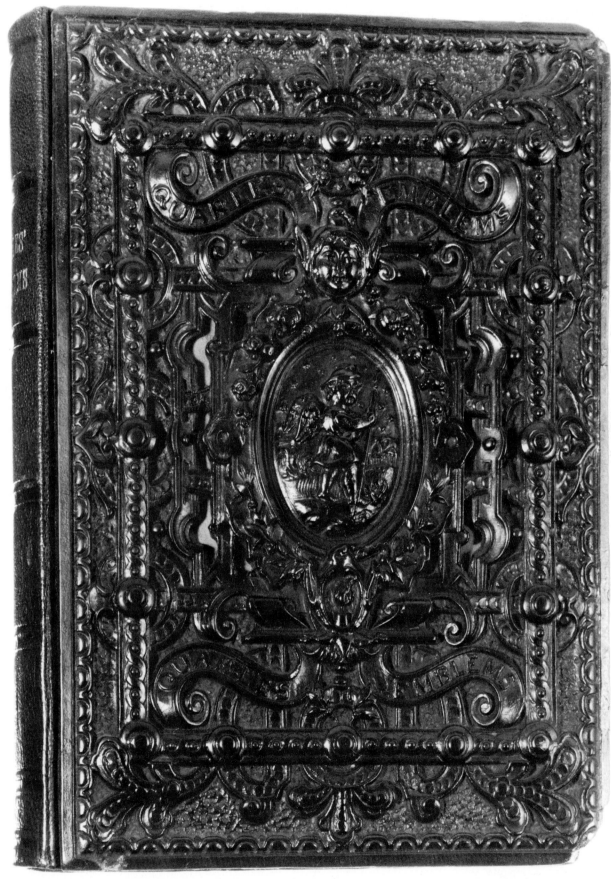

Quarles' Emblems
Illustrated by Charles Bennett and
W. Harry Rogers
Nisbet, 1861
230 × 155 mm

Black papier-mâché, with papier-mâché spine. The design has been adapted from *Sentiments and Similes*.
Collection R. de Beaumont

The Origin and Progress of the Art of Writing
Henry Noel Humphreys
Day & Son, 1855 (2nd edition)
267×180 mm

Black papier-mâché on crimson paper. First edition, in papier-mâché, was published by Ingram, Cooke & Co. in 1852 and sold at 1 guinea (ECB).
Massey College, Toronto, H32

The Coinage of the British Empire
Henry Noel Humphreys
Griffin, 1863 (3rd edition)
c. 257 × 162 mm

Black papier-mâché on scarlet paper, exactly as first edition published by Bogue in 1855, with black leather spine, gold blocked, with different design. The covers show the Royal Arms as used by Henry VII, Henry VIII and Edward VI, and the panel below the central shield bears the monogram 'HR' (Henricus Rex).
Massey College, Toronto, H36

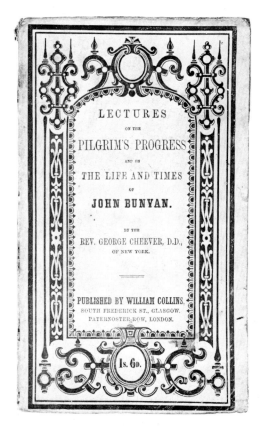

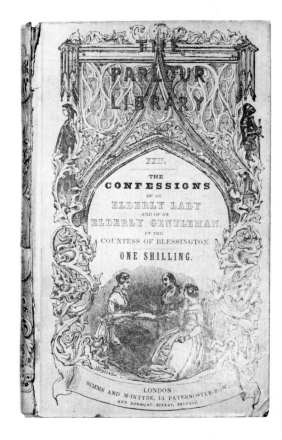

Nelson's British Library
Thomas Nelson, n.d. [1840s]
172 × 106 mm

Paper on boards, printed from wood in red, yellow and blue.
Collection R. de Beaumont

Poetical Works of Sir Walter Scott
Simms & McIntyre, 1846
180 × 118 mm

Paper, lithographed in gold, blue and black.
Collection R. de Beaumont

Lectures on the Pilgrim's Progress etc.
Rev. G. Cheever
Wm Collins, 1846
188 × 114 mm

Paper, printed from type and wood in blue.
Collection R. de Beaumont

The Confessions etc.
Vol. XXII in The Parlour Library
Simms & McIntyre, 1848
172 × 118 mm

Paper, printed from wood in red-brown on green paper. Cover design by H. Warren, cut by W. Dickes.

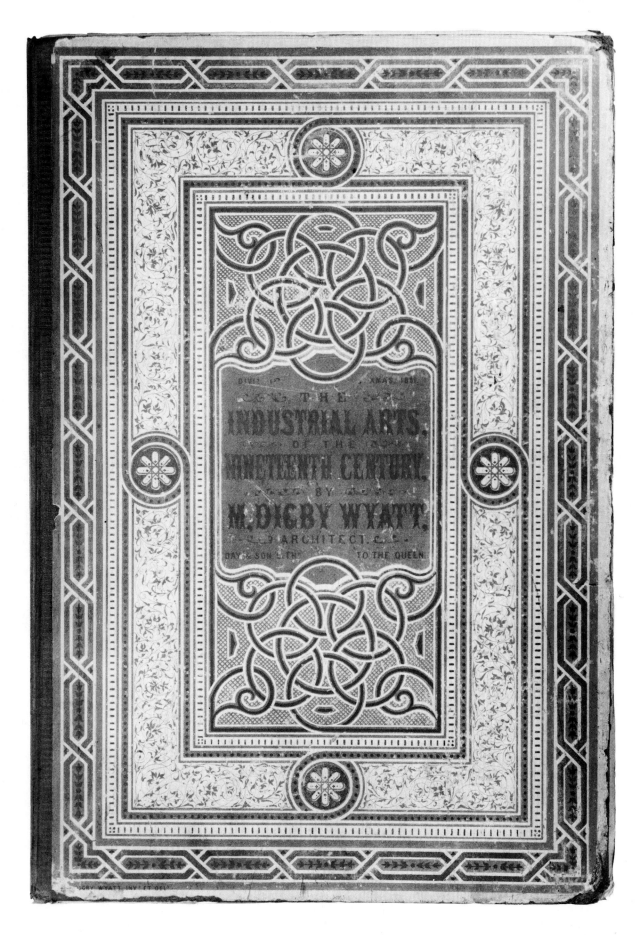

The Industrial Arts of the Nineteenth Century
M. Digby Wyatt
Day & Son, 1851
Cover of the first part issue, Xmas 1851
494 × 330 mm

Paper on boards, cloth spine, lithographed in mauve and bronze over buff underprint, on pale yellow paper. Design by M. Digby Wyatt. *Collection V. Ridler*

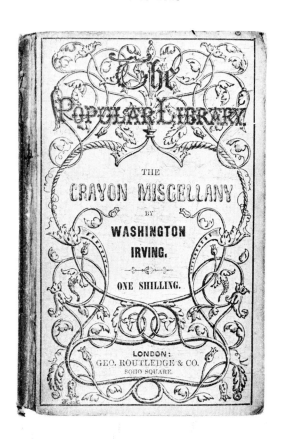

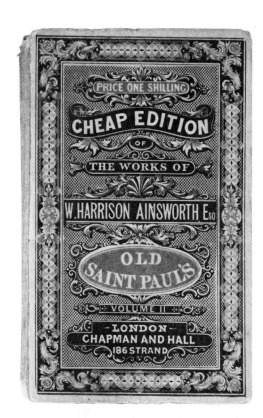

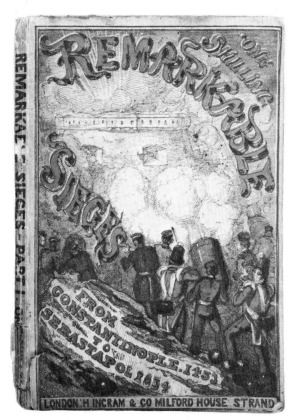

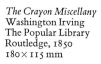

The Crayon Miscellany
Washington Irving
The Popular Library
Routledge, 1850
180 × 115 mm

Paper on boards, printed in blue from type and wood on emerald green paper.

Old Saint Paul's
W. Harrison Ainsworth
Chapman & Hall, 1850
175 × 110 mm

Yellow paper on boards, printed in red and blue using bank-note design technique, possibly by compound plates (two colours at one impression) by Whiting, who took over the Congreve compound plate process.
Private collection

Remarkable Sieges
Henry Ottley
H. Ingram, 1854
186 × 125 mm

Paper, printed from wood in red, blue and black by Edmund Evans. Sold at 1s. (ECB).
Massey College, Toronto, PB91

A Story with a Vengeance
Nathaniel Cooke, n.d. [before 1856]
190 × 128 mm

Paper, printed in red and blue by Edmund Evans; design perhaps by Charles Keene.
Collection R. de Beaumont

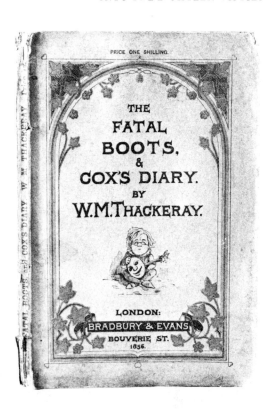

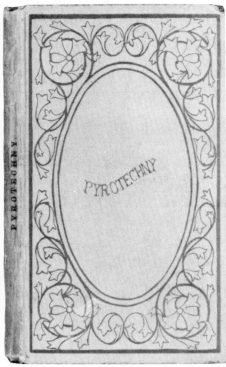

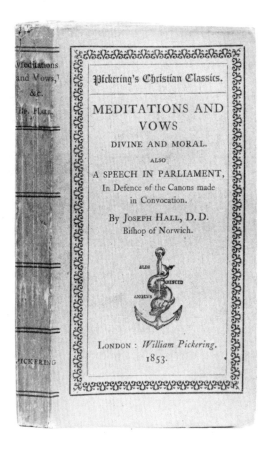

Language of the Eye
Joseph Turnley
Illustrated by Gilbert & Anelay
Partridge, 1856
190 × 128 mm

Yellow paper, printed in gold, red and green.
Collection R. de Beaumont

The Fatal Boots, & Cox's Diary
W. M. Thackeray
Bradbury & Evans, 1855
189 × 126 mm

Yellow paper, printed in black from type and woodblock, signed 'H. Leighton sc.' Sold at 1s.

Pyrotechny; or, a familiar system of recreative fire-works
G. W. Mortimer
London, James S. Hodson, n.d.
[1852] (2nd edition)
190 × 113 mm

Yellow paper on boards, printed in red on front, spine and back. The title is repeated on the spine. All illustrated guide to making fireworks, printed by the publisher.
Private Collection

Meditations and Vows Divine and Moral etc.
Joseph Hall
Reprinted for W. Pickering, 1851
142 × 75 mm

Green paper on card, printed in black on upper, spine and lower. One of 'Pickering's Christian Classics', in elegant Chiswick Press typography: the cover (similar to, but not identical with, the title-page) is dated 1853.
Collection John Porter

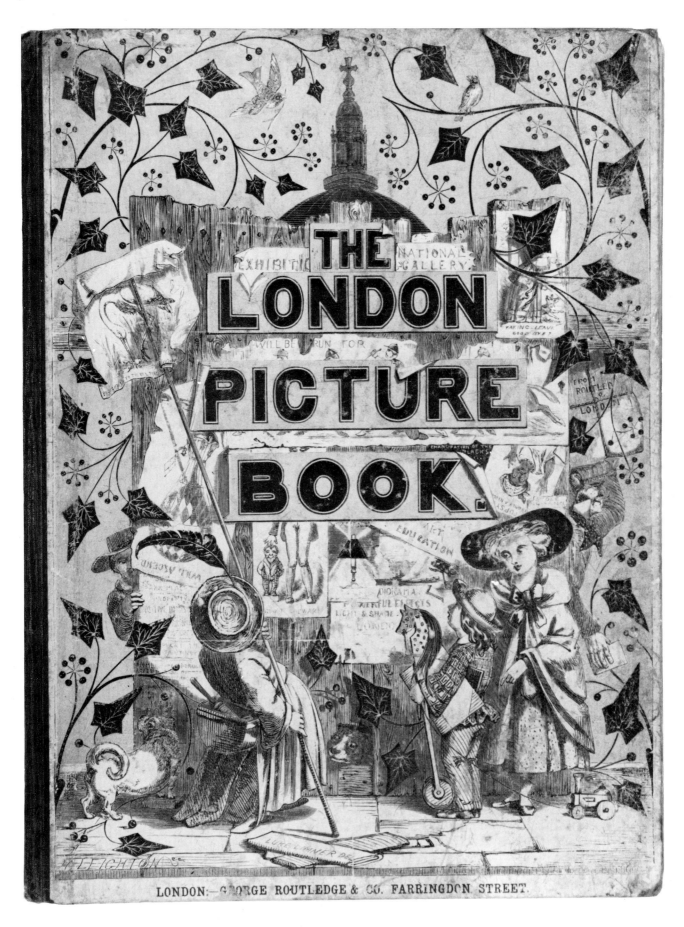

The London Picture Book for all Good Boys and Girls
Routledge, 1853
330 × 245 mm

Glazed pink paper on boards, cloth spine. Printed from wood in blue and black; designed by Luke Limner (John Leighton), cut by Leighton. Among the items pasted on the hoarding (behind the book's title) are references to 'Topsy' and 'Emancipation of the Blacks': *Uncle Tom's Cabin* was published in London in 1852. Sold at 5s. (ECB).
Massey College, Toronto, PB85

The Days, Months, and Seasons of the Year
Maria Jacob
Nathaniel Cooke, 1853
188 × 176 mm

Card, printed in four colours from wood by Edmund Evans.
Private Collection

The Bayeux Tapestry Elucidated
Rev. J. Collingwood Bruce
John Russell Smith, 1856
288 × 214 mm

Glazed paper on boards, red leather
spine, partly gilt. The rich cover
designs, unsigned, are chromolithographed in green, blue, red, black and
gold on cream paper. Sold at 1 guinea
(ECB).
Massey College, Toronto, PB72

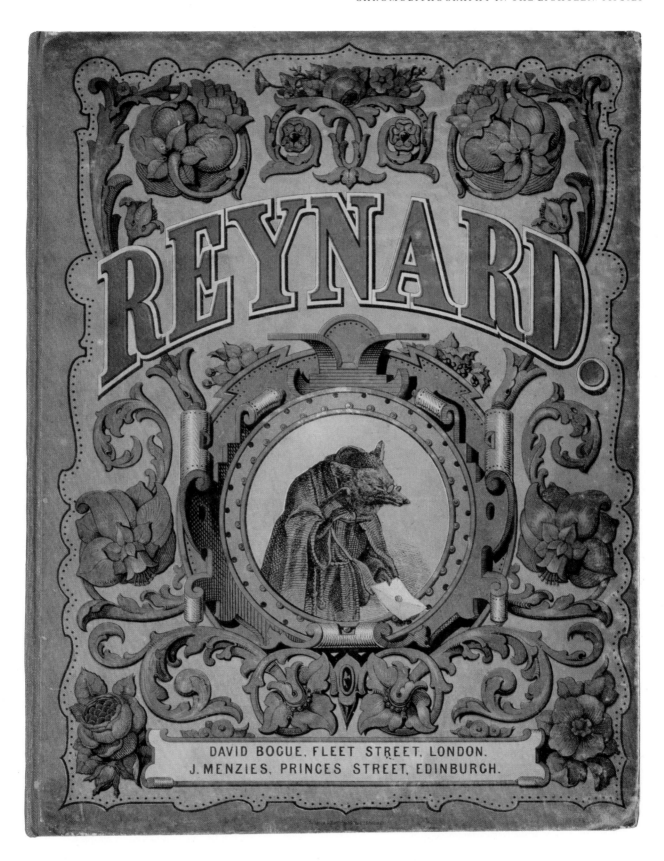

Reynard the Fox
David Vedder
Ill. Gustav Canton
David Bogue, n.d. (first published
1852)
267 × 210 mm

Paper on boards, cloth spine. The
design, same upper and lower, is
lithographed in green, gold, pink,
grey and black by Schenck &
McFarlane, Edinburgh.
Private Collection

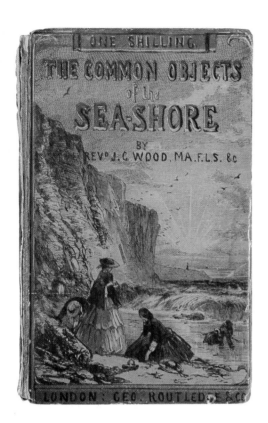

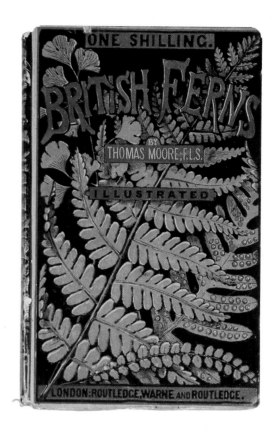

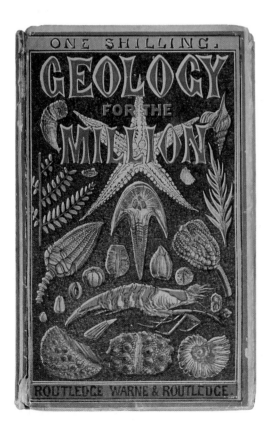

The Common Objects of the Sea Shore
J. C. Wood
Ill. G. B. Sowerby
Routledge, 1858
168 × 104 mm

Yellow paper on boards, printed in red, green and black from wood by Edmund Evans.

British Ferns
T. Moore
Ill. W. S. Coleman
Routledge, Warne & Routledge, 1860
170 × 106 mm

Yellow paper on boards, printed in red, black and green from wood by Edmund Evans.
Private Collection

Geology for the Million
Margaret Plues
Routledge, Warne & Routledge, 1863
170 × 106 mm

Yellow paper on boards, printed in red, green and black from wood by Edmund Evans.
Private Collection

British Birds' Eggs and Nests
Rev. J. C. Atkinson
Ill. W. S. Coleman
Routledge, n.d. [1860s]
164 × 102 mm

Yellow paper on boards, printed in red, green and black from wood by Camden Press (Dalziel Brothers).

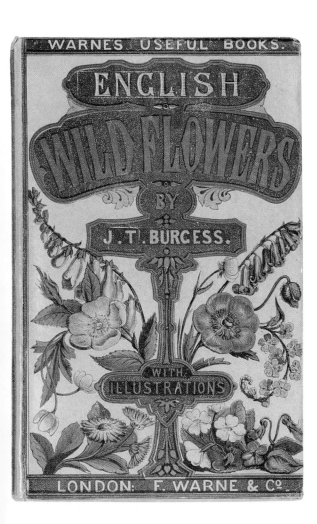

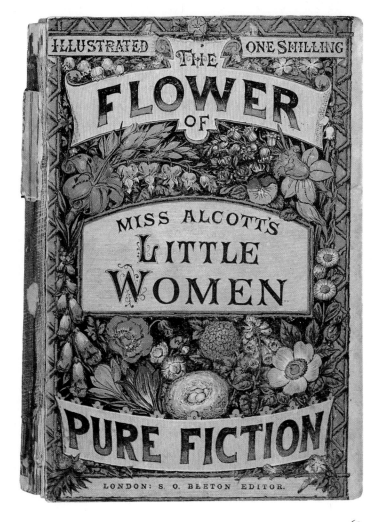

English Wild Flowers
J. T. Burgess
Warne, n.d. [1860s]
170 × 105 mm

Pink paper on boards, printed in red,
blue and green by Camden Press.
Private Collection

Little Women
Louisa Alcott
Goubaud & Son, n.d. [*c.*1870]
174 × 120 mm

Paper on boards, printed in red, blue,
yellow, green and black by Leighton
Bros.
Collection Don Parkinson

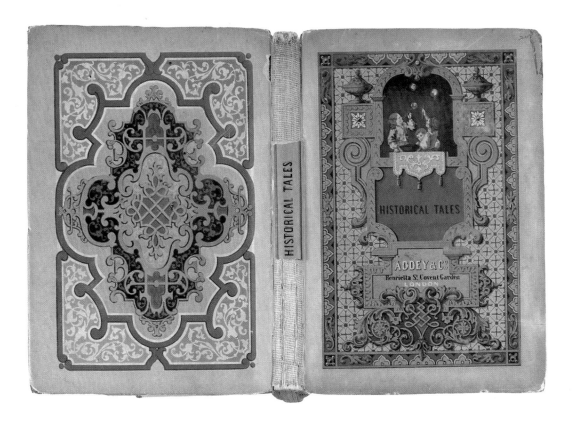

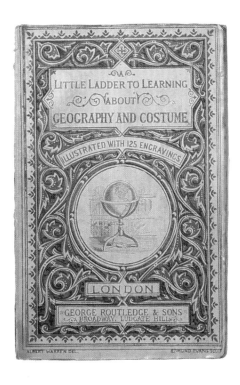

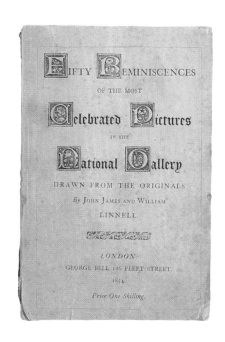

Historical Tales
M.J.
Ill. George Thomas
Addey & Co., n.d. [*c.*1856]
202 × 140 mm

Paper on boards, chromolithographed in green, yellow, blue, red,
gold, buff and black. One of a series
of books for children, each with a
different, richly chromolithographed,
non-figurative cover design.
Collection Don Parkinson

*A Little Ladder to Learning, about
Geography and Costume*
Routledge, n.d. [*c.*1870]
184 × 120 mm

Yellow paper, printed in red and
green from wood by Edmund Evans.
Cover design by Albert Warren.
This series was originated by Joseph
Cundall.
Private Collection

Hand-Book for the National Gallery
Felix Summerly (Henry Cole)
Ill. J. J. and W. Linnell
George Bell, 1854
162 × 108 mm

Buff paper printed from type and
woodblock, probably by Chiswick
Press.
Massey College, Toronto, PB92

The Cathedral, or Abbey Church of Iona
Messrs. Buckley and the Bishop of
Argyll
Day & Son, 1866
285 × 220 mm

Paper on boards, cloth spine, chromolithographed in red, yellow, blue,
green, pink, ochre and black by Day
& Son.

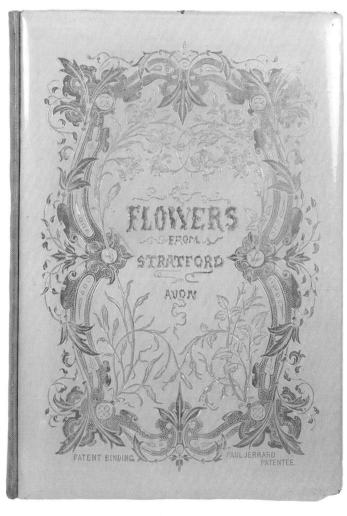

The Floral Offering
Paul Jerrard, n.d. [1860s]
277 × 184 mm

Paper with chromolithographed design laid on cloth boards inside gold-blocked rule, on upper only.
Private Collection

Flowers from Stratford on Avon
Paul Jerrard, n.d. [1860s]
280 × 192 mm

'Porcelain' binding: i.e. boards coated (laminated?) with a shiny composition substance, blocked in gold on upper; leather spine.
Private Collection

These books were advertised as 'Paul Jerrard's Cream and Gold Special Presents' and were expensive: *The Floral Offering*, as above, was 21s., the *Flowers* was priced at 31s.6d.

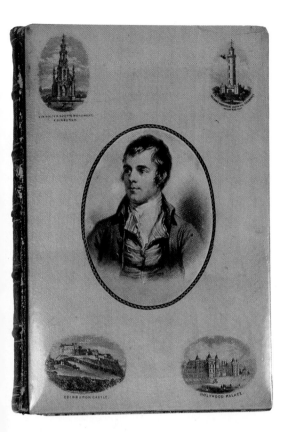

The Poetical Works and Letters of Robert Burns
Gall & Inglis, n.d. [1860s–70s]
188 × 120 mm

Mauchline binding, the oval engraving of Burns on the upper, and an oval photograph on the lower, are paper cut-outs stuck down on the wood cover beneath the (?) shellac glaze. The engravings in the corners were transferred by the method described by E. & E. Pinto in *Tunbridge and Scottish Souvenir Woodware*, Bell, 1970, p.111 (see p.14). The lower cover is fitted with four mother-of-pearl studs to lift it from the surface on which it is placed. Leather spine, all edges gilt.
Private Collection

The Complete Poetical Works of Robert Burns
John Walker, n.d. [1860s–70s]
185 × 124 mm

Bevelled boards coated with shiny substance apparently similar to *Flowers from Stratford on Avon*, facing. Chromolithographed design on upper cover is on paper pasted down inside gold border, beneath lamination: the word 'Burns' blocked in gold on top. Leather spine blocked in gold.
Private Collection

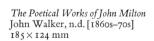

Chips from Dickens
Selected by Thomas Mason
David Bryce, Glasgow, n.d. [1860s–70s]
90 × 58 mm

Mauchline binding, oval photograph pasted on wood upper, plain wood lower, cloth spine blocked in gold.
Private Collection

The Poetical Works of John Milton
John Walker, n.d. [1860s–70s]
185 × 124 mm

Mauchline binding, the upper cover is chromolithographed paper stuck down over wood: the lower is plain wood. Both covers have been 'glazed' with shellac and the upper blocked in gold with the word 'Milton' (on the vase). Leather spine, all edges gilt.
Private Collection

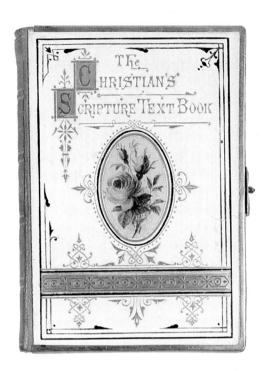

The Christian's Scripture Text Book
G. T. Godwin, n.d. [1860s]
126 × 85 mm

Ivory paper on boards with brass
edging and clasp, printed in colour
and blocked in gold on upper;
leather spine, a.e.g.
Private Collection

The Beauties of Shakespeare
Rev. William Dodd
Routledge, n.d. (inscribed 1876)
178 × 110 mm

Ivory paper on boards with brass
edging, printed in blue, red, green
and black, blocked in gold, on upper;
leather spine, a.e.g.
Private Collection

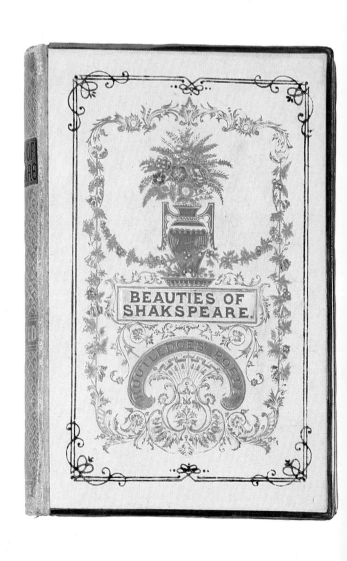

Uncle Buncle's New Stories about
Animals
Dean & Co., n.d. [c.1845]
208 × 165 mm

Buff paper, printed in black. The
delicate, academic drawing on the
cover, reproduced by lithography,
has little in common with the cruder,
hand-coloured illustrations inside.
Private Collection

Uncle Buncle's Pretty Tales
Dean & Co., n.d. [c.1850]
208 × 165 mm

The hand-coloured illustrations inside are more fun than this poorly
drawn cover.
Private Collection

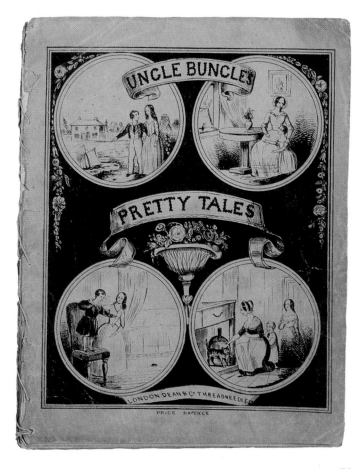

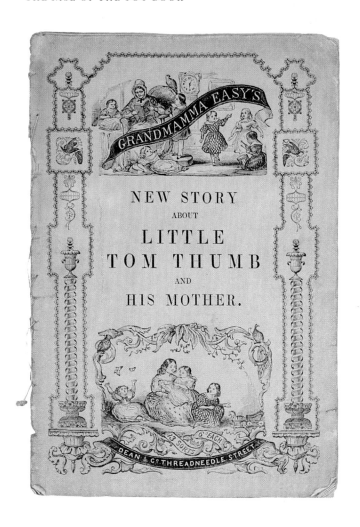

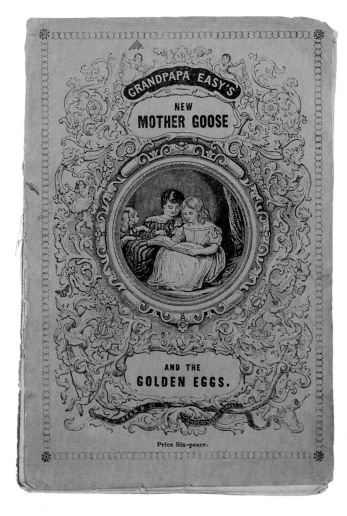

Grandmamma Easy's New Story etc.
Dean & Co., n.d. [*c.*1845]
244 × 168 mm

Woodcut decoration and illustration
on cover, hand-coloured woodcut
illustrations inside.
Private Collection

*Grandpapa Easy's New Mother Goose
and the Golden Eggs*
Dean & Co., n.d. [*c.*1845]
244 × 168 mm

Mauve paper, woodcut decoration
and illustration on cover, elaborate
hand-coloured woodcut illustrations
inside.
Private Collection

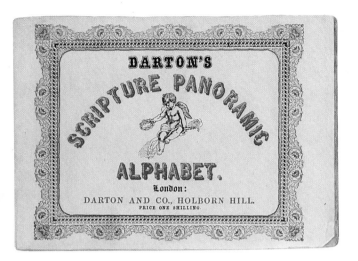

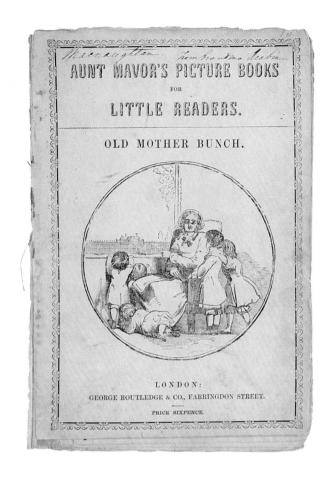

Darton's Scripture Panoramic Alphabet
Darton & Co., n.d. [1850s]
135 × 190 mm

Paper, cover printed in red and black
from type and woodcut ornament:
inside illustrations printed from wood
in black and two (varying) colours.

*Aunt Mavor's Picture Books: Old
Mother Bunch's Day at the Great
Exhibition*
Routledge, n.d. [1851]
235 × 165 mm

Paper, the crude illustrations inside
are hand-coloured.

Happy Children
Darton & Hodge, n.d. [c.1862]
260 × 180 mm

Pink glazed paper, printed in red and
blue from wood: illustrations inside
crudely colour-printed from wood.

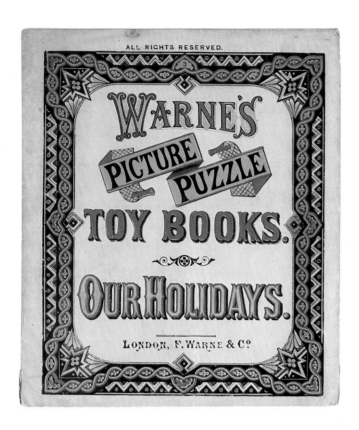

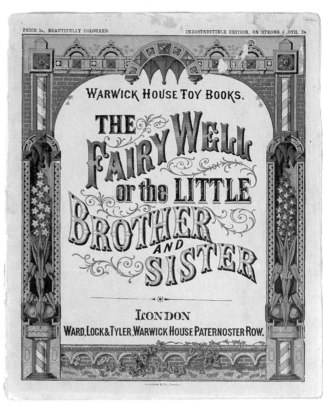

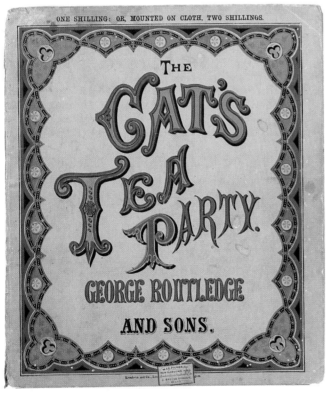

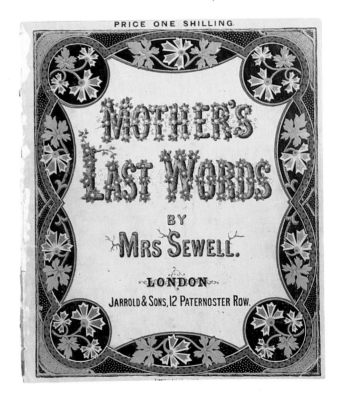

Our Holidays
F. Warne, n.d. (inscribed 1883)
268 × 233 mm

Yellow card, 'Fairground' lettering printed in red, blue, chrome and black, probably by Kronheim.

The Fairy Well etc.
Ward, Lock & Tyler, n.d. [1870s]
272 × 227 mm

Pink card, 'Fairground' lettering and decoration, printed in red, blue, yellow, green and black, by Kronheim.

The Cat's Tea Party
Routledge, n.d. [c.1870]
267 × 232 mm

Pink card, printed in red, blue, yellow, green and black by Kronheim.

Mother's Last Words
Mrs Sewell
Jarrold & Sons, n.d. [1870s]
255 × 218 mm

Yellow card, printed in red, blue, ochre and black by Kronheim.

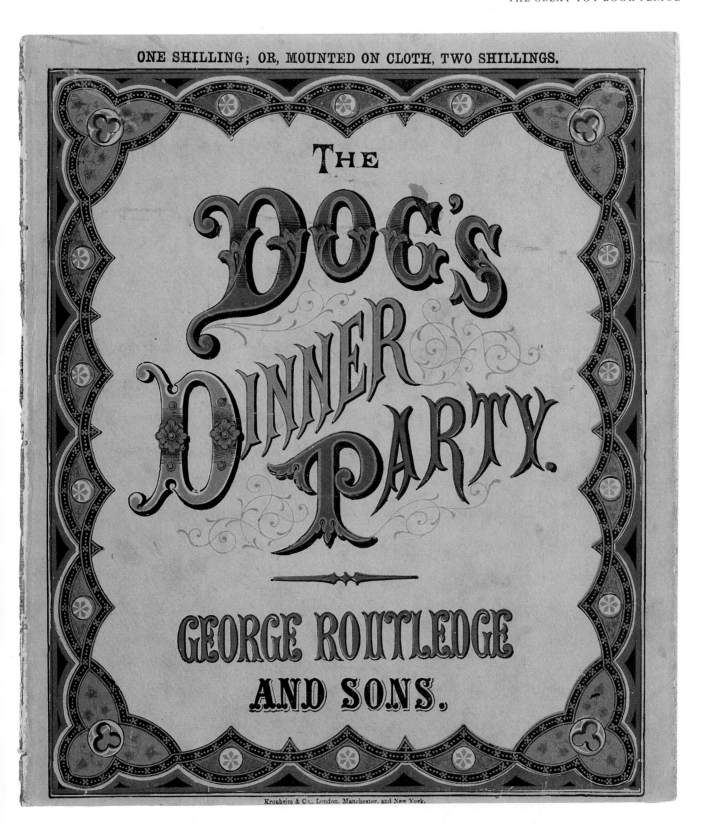

ONE SHILLING; OR, MOUNTED ON CLOTH, TWO SHILLINGS.

THE
Dog's
Dinner Party.

GEORGE ROUTLEDGE
AND SONS.

Kronheim & Co., London, Manchester, and New York.

The Dog's Dinner Party
Routledge, n.d. [*c.*1870]
268 × 227 mm

Pink card, printed by Kronheim, no.45 in Routledge's Shilling Toy books. Illustrations inside by Harrison Weir. 'Fairground style' lettering.

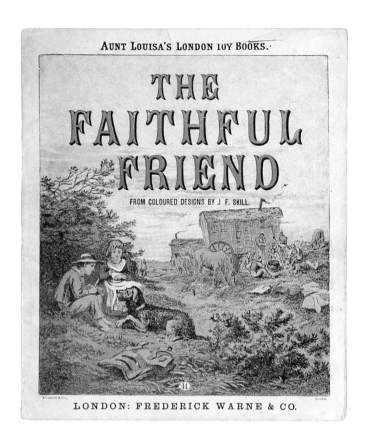

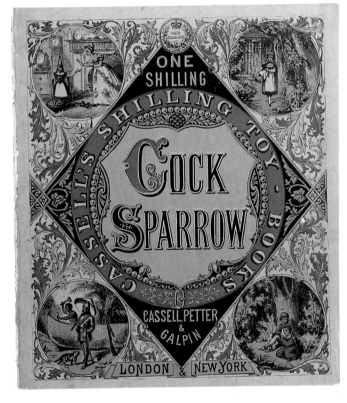

The Faithful Friend
Warne, n.d. [1870s]
266 × 230 mm

Glazed card, no.41 in Aunt Louisa's
London Toy Books. Printed by
Kronheim. Illustrated by J. F. Skill.
This cover design is probably earlier
than the other.
Private Collection

The Faithful Friend
Warne, n.d. [1870s]
262 × 225 mm

Mauve card printed by Kronheim,
no.41 in Aunt Louisa's London Toy
Books. The artist's name has been
omitted from this cover.

The Robin's Christmas Eve
Warne, n.d. [c.1869]
255 × 220 mm

Yellow card, printed by Kronheim,
no.11 in Aunt Louisa's London Toy
Books. Lettering and decorations in
the fairground tradition.

Cock Sparrow
Cassell, Petter & Galpin, n.d. [c.1870]
260 × 225 mm

Mauve card, printed letterpress in
colours. An odd mixture of decorative styles. The shilling at the top is
dated 1868. This title was no.1 in
Cassell's Shilling Toy Book Series.

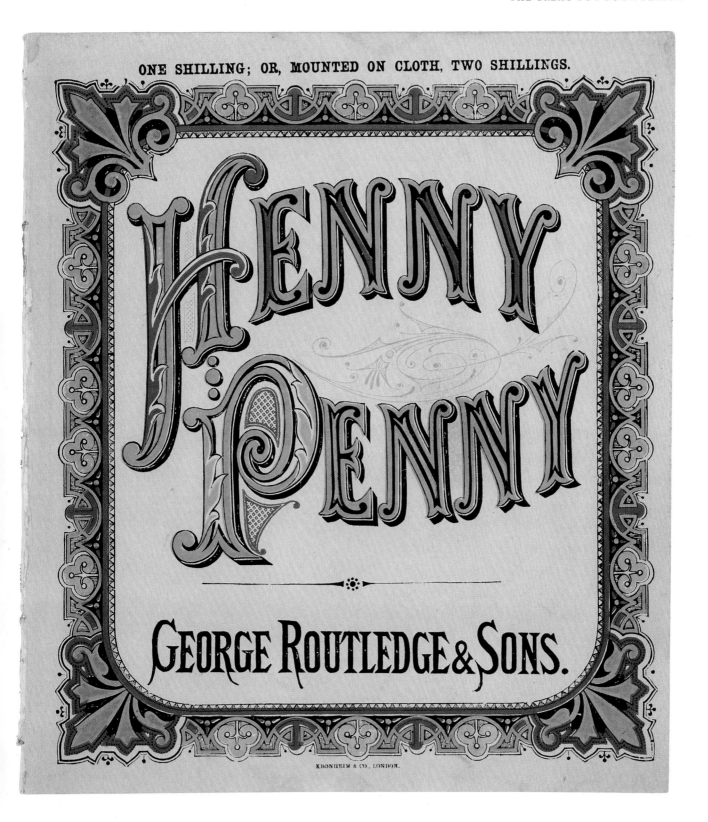

Henny Penny
Routledge, n.d. [1870s]
260 × 225 mm

Yellow card printed letterpress in red,
blue, yellow and black by Kronheim.
A delightful example of fairground
style decoration.

The Pet Lamb
J. B. Darton & Hodge, n.d. [1860s]
270 × 185 mm

Yellow paper on card, printed from wood in red, green and black. This book is described in *Osborne*, vol. 2, p.694, and dated *c*.1850, but this copy must be dated 1860s, since the imprint 'Darton & Hodge' dates from 1862 (*Osborne*, vol. 2, p.472). The illustrations (printed in colour from woodblocks) are signed 'Calvert'.

Morning, Noon and Night
P. H. Drake & Co., New York, 1871
208 × 140 mm

Paper, printed from wood in four colours and black. It is stated inside that this 'Medical Annual', in its third year, is printed in an edition of 6,000,000 copies at a cost of $120,000, and that it was intended to give one away with every bottle of 'Plantation Bitters' (a 'vegetable restorative' promoted by the booklet), but the sale of bottles during the period of the booklet, 1871–2, will exceed 7,000,000.
Private Collection

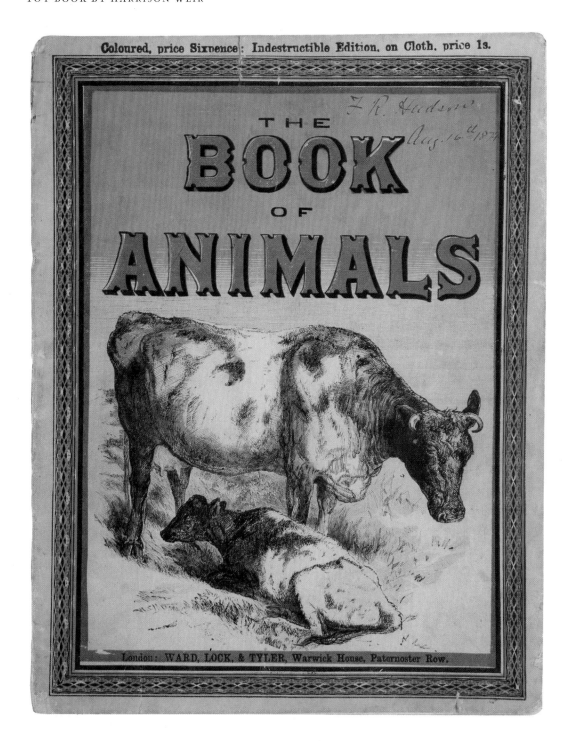

The Book of Animals
Ward, Lock & Tyler, n.d. (inscribed
1874)
240 × 186 mm

Yellow paper, printed by Edmund
Evans in blue, red and black. Illustrations by Harrison Weir.

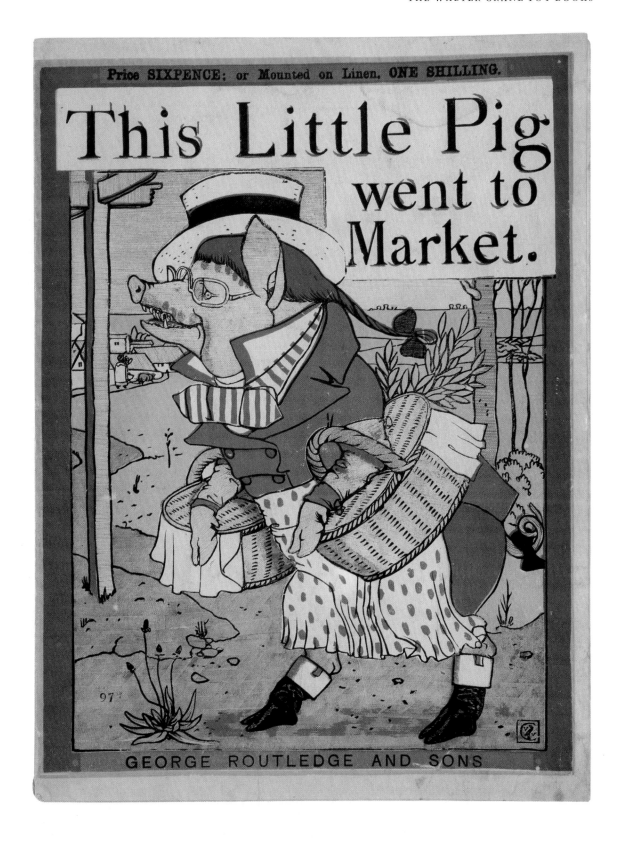

This Little Pig Went to Market
Walter Crane
Routledge, n.d. [1870]
248 × 185 mm

Card, printed in green, red and black
by Edmund Evans. No.97 in Rout-
ledge's New Sixpenny Toy Books.
The seventh of Walter Crane's Toy
Books.
Private Collection

The Babes in the Wood
Routledge, n.d. [1879]
232 × 207 mm

Card, printed in four colours by
Edmund Evans. The fourth of Ran-
dolph Caldecott's Picture Books.
Private Collection

The Fox jumps over the Parson's Gate
Routledge, n.d. [1883]
203 × 240 mm

Card, printed in four colours by
Edmund Evans. The twelfth of
Caldecott's Picture Books.

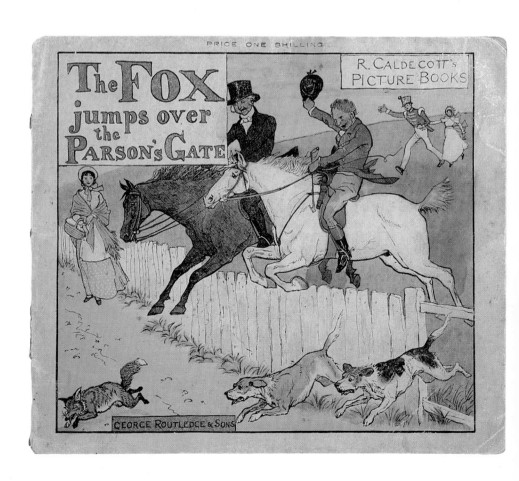

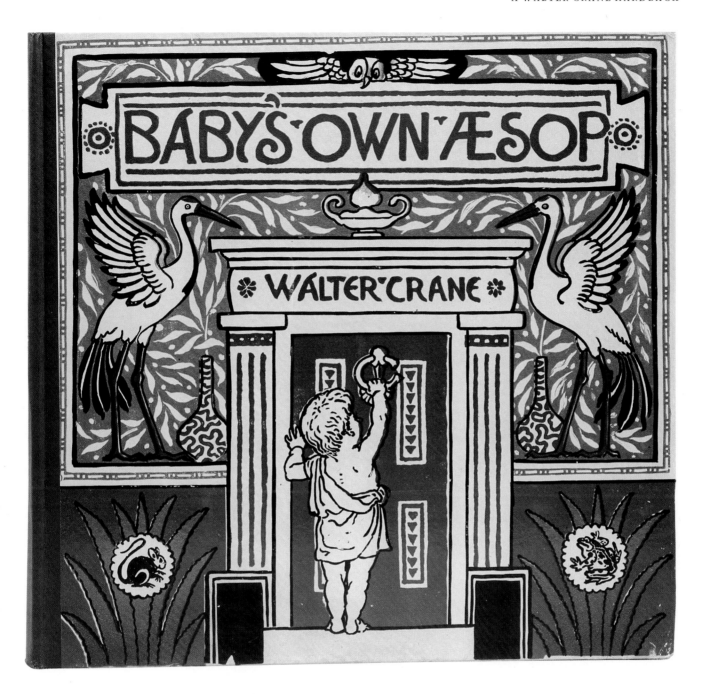

The Baby's own Aesop
Walter Crane
Warne, n.d. [1887]
182 × 192 mm

Paper on boards, cloth spine. Printed
in green, red and black by Edmund
Evans. The Japanese and 'art nouveau'
influence is evident.
Private Collection

The Princess Nobody
Longmans, Green, n.d. [1884]
242 × 188 mm

Glazed paper on boards, cloth spine,
printed in colours by Edmund Evans.
The illustrations are by 'Dicky'
Doyle.
Private Collection

A Toy Book by 'Phiz'
Routledge, n.d. [1883]
244 × 190 mm

Paper on boards, cloth spine, printed
in five colours by Edmund Evans.
The sunflower part of the design
appears to be signed AME; the two
children are by 'Phiz' (H. K. Browne).
Private Collection

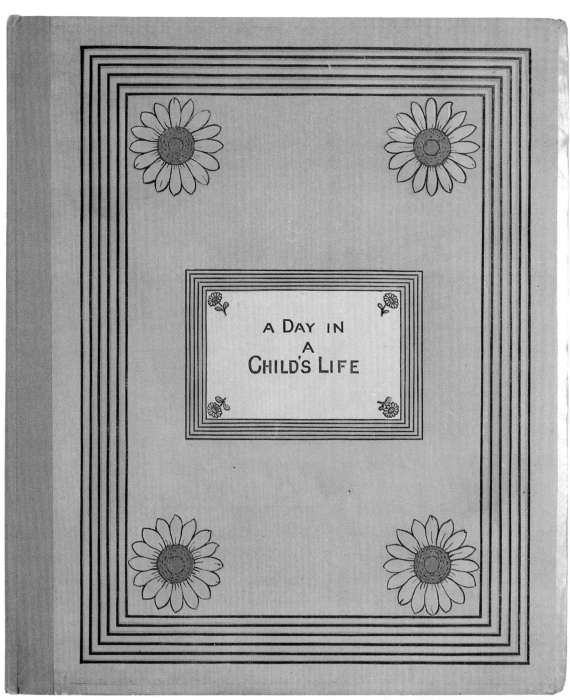

A Day in a Child's Life
Routledge, n.d. [1881]
250 × 214 mm

Glazed toned paper on bevelled
boards, cloth spine, printed in brown,
yellow and green by Edmund Evans.
The sunflowers on the cover echo one
of the illustrations inside by Kate
Greenaway. Was this sophisticated
cover actually designed by K.G.?
Some years later, the book appeared
with a different, pictorial, cover
[right].
Private Collection

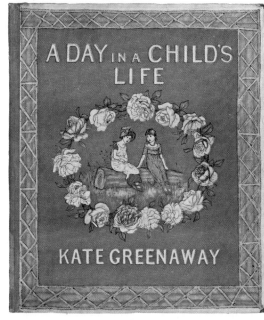

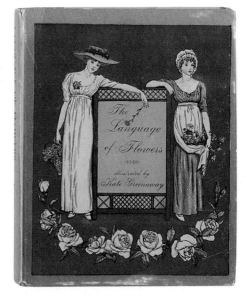

The Pied Piper of Hamelin
Routledge, n.d. [1889]
256 × 224 mm

Glazed paper on boards, cloth spine,
printed in green, yellow, red, blue,
grey and black by Edmund Evans:
illustration by Kate Greenaway.
Private Collection

The Language of Flowers
Routledge, n.d. [1884]
150 × 120 mm

Glazed paper on boards, cloth spine,
printed in red, yellow, green, grey
and black by Edmund Evans. Illustration by Kate Greenaway.
Private Collection

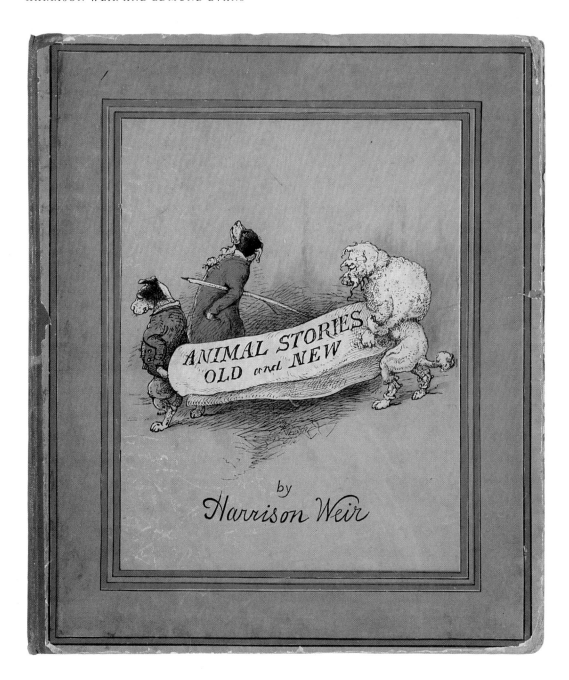

Animal Stories Old and New
Sampson Low, etc., n.d. [1885]
255 × 216 mm

Glazed paper on boards, cloth spine,
printed in red, orange, blue, green
and black by Edmund Evans. Illustration by Harrison Weir.
Collection Fianach Lawry

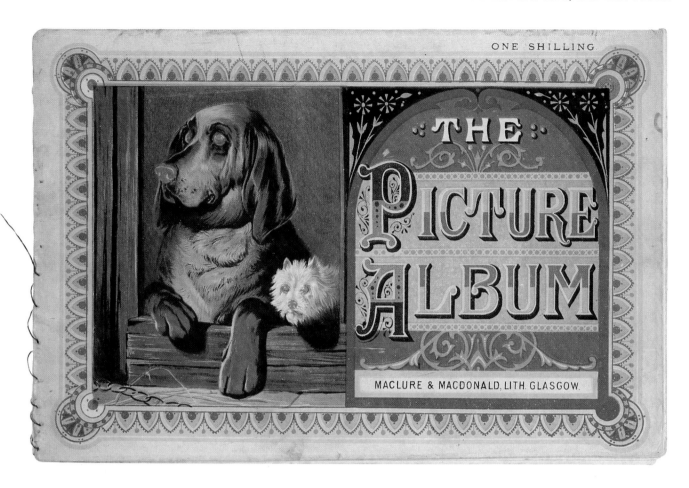

ONE SHILLING

"THE"

Picture Album

MACLURE & MACDONALD, LITH. GLASGOW.

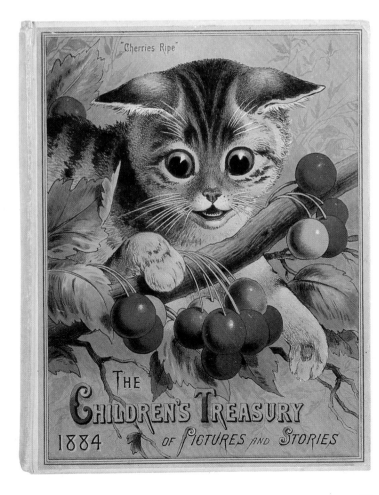

"Cherries Ripe"

THE CHILDREN'S TREASURY
1884   OF PICTURES AND STORIES

The Picture Album
MacLure & Macdonald, Glasgow,
n.d. [1880s]
180 × 275 mm

Card. Chromolithography of a
dubious artistic standard by Maclure
& Macdonald.
Private Collection

*The Children's Treasury of Pictures and
Stories*
T. Nelson (inscribed 1883), 1884
190 × 150 mm

Glazed paper upper cover illustration
pasted down on paper on boards. The
quality of the chromolithographed
colour is excellent.

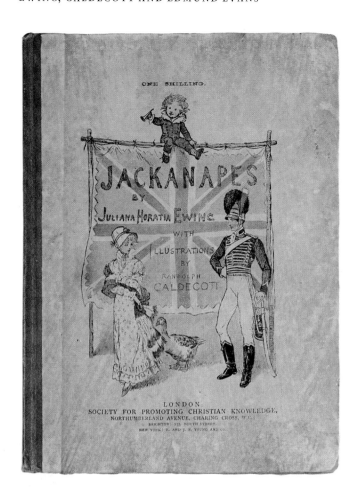

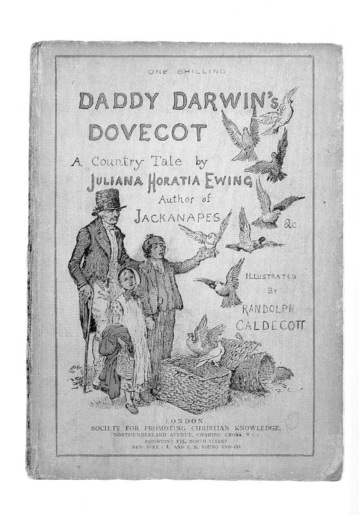

Jackanapes
S.P.C.K., n.d. [1884]
213 × 160 mm

Buff paper on boards, cloth spine,
printed in blue, red and black by
Edmund Evans; illustration by R.
Caldecott.

Daddy Darwin's Dovecot
S.P.C.K., n.d. [1884]
213 × 160 mm

Toned paper on boards, printed in
red and black by Edmund Evans;
illustration by R. Caldecott.

*Blue & Red: or the Discontented
Lobster*
Juliana Horatia Ewing
Illustrated by R. André
S.P.C.K., n.d. [1883]
238 × 182 mm

Chromolithographed paper (by Emrik & Binger, London) on boards
(same design upper and lower), red
cloth spine.
Private Collection

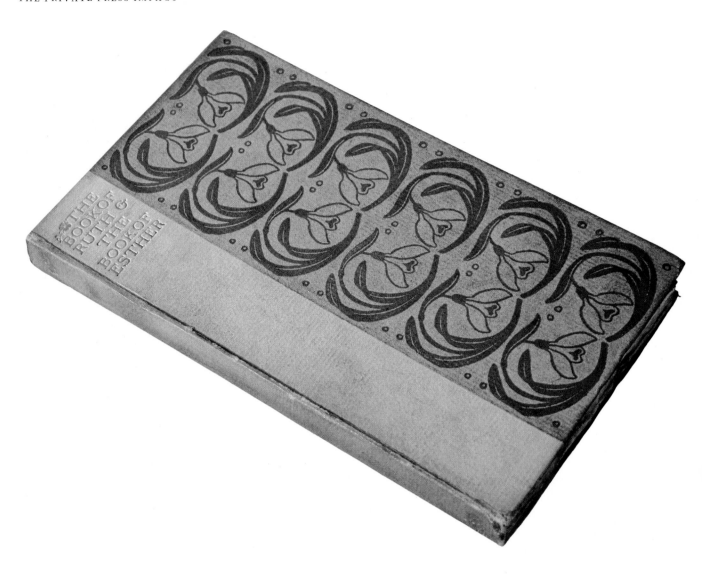

The Book of Ruth & the Book of Esther
Printed and illustrated by Lucien
Pissarro (Eragny Press), Epping,
Essex, in an edition of 155 copies.
150 copies for sale by Hacon &
Ricketts, 1896
172 × 100 mm

Handmade paper spine blocked in
gold, green paper sides printed in
green.
National Library of Scotland

A Bunch of Heartsease
165 mm deep
n.d. [1890s]

'Any mother desiring another copy of "A Bunch of Heartsease" can obtain it by writing to Scott & Bowne Ltd, 10 & 11 Stonecutter Street, Ludgate Circus, London EC.' Also a free sample bottle of Scott's Emulsion by forwarding 3d. for postage. Paper, printed by chromolithography, and cut out.
Private Collection

This Little Pig
Illustrated by E. Caldwell
Marcus Ward, n.d. [1890s]
178 mm deep

Paper, printed by chromolithography, and cut out.
Private Collection

Seaside Memories
Drawings by A. Wilde Parsons
Ernest Nister, n.d. [1890s]
135 × 90 mm

Card chromolithographed by Nister in Nuremberg, die-stamped in blind and gold and cut out. The back is illustrated on p.15.
Collection R. de Beaumont

A Flower Girl
Helen J. Wood
Ernest Nister, n.d. [1890s]
135 mm deep

Card, printed by chromolithography in Bavaria, and cut out.
Private Collection

M. or N.
G. J. Whyte-Melville
Chapman & Hall, 1872
186 × 120 mm

Yellow glazed paper on boards printed from wood in red and blue. Sold at 2s. The yellow-back style flourished for half a century.
Private Collection

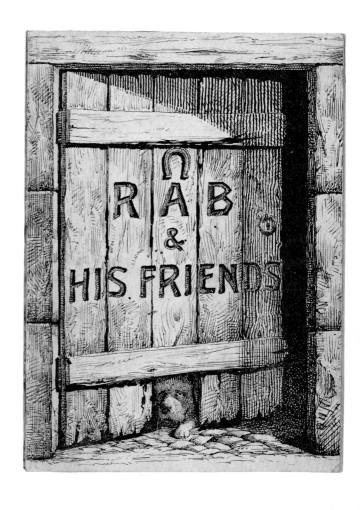

Rab and his friends
John Brown
Edinburgh, David Douglas, 1877
184 × 135 mm

Blue glazed paper on card lithographed in black on upper cover only. The cover illustration is unsigned: a wood-engraved portrait of 'Rab', the mastiff, on the title-page, is signed J. ADAM [an Edinburgh wood-engraver] and EDWIN DOUGLAS. Printed in Edinburgh by T. & A. Constable.
Private Collection

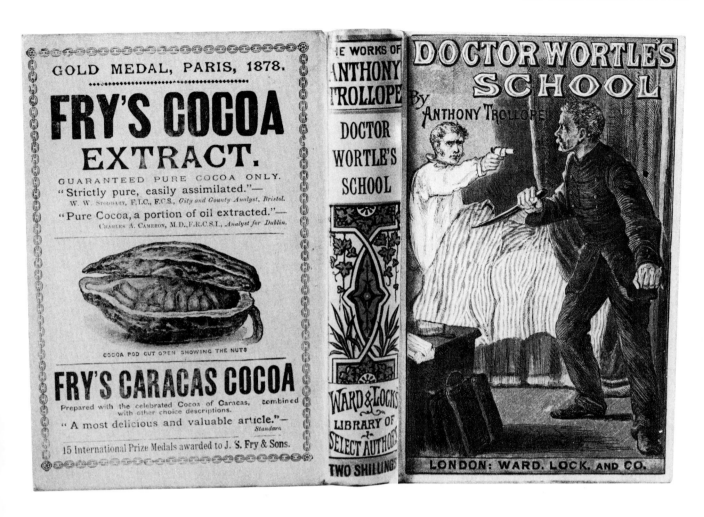

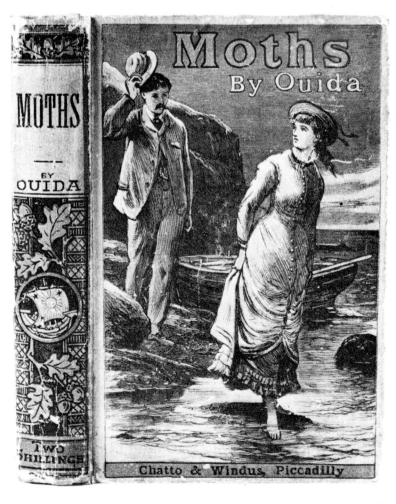

Dr Wortle's School
Anthony Trollope
Ward, Lock & Co., n.d.
(advertisement at back dated 1889)
178 × 118 mm

White glazed paper on boards, printed from type and wood in dark blue, light blue and red (by Edmund Evans?).

Moths
Ouida
Chatto & Windus, 1892
177 × 118 mm

Yellow glazed paper on boards, printed from wood in red and blue. Sold at 2s.

The Tiny Lawn Tennis Club
by the Designer of the Children's
Kettledrum
Dean & Son, n.d. (inscribed 1884)
226 × 180 mm

Chromolithographed paper on
boards, brown cloth spine. The illustrations are Kate Greenaway-ish, but
slightly less stilted.
Private Collection

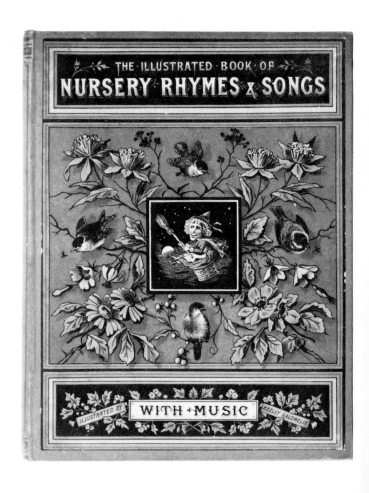

*The Illustrated Book of Nursery
Rhymes and Songs*
Illustrated by Keeley Halswelle
T. Nelson, 1882
207 × 156 mm

Dark yellow cloth, with colour-
printed paper pasted on upper cover,
spine and lower cover blocked in red.
Private Collection

The Snow Queen
Hans Christian Andersen
Illustrated by T. Pym
No publisher, n.d. [1883]
211 × 182 mm

Paper on boards, chromolithographed, different picture on upper
and lower, blue cloth spine.
Private Collection

Gulliver's Travels
Frederick Warne, 1887
274 × 225 mm

Paper on boards, chromolithographed by Emrik & Binger, London, blue cloth spine. Printed by
Dalziel Bros.
Private Collection

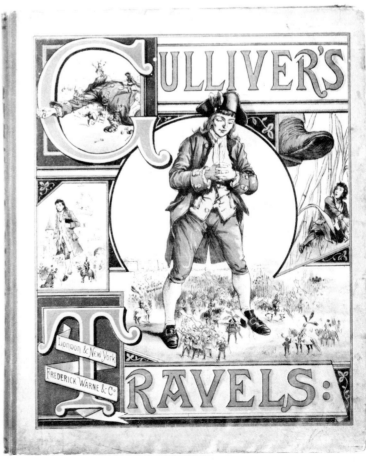

Light in the Gloaming
by the author of 'One of these Little
Ones'
S.P.C.K., 1882
148 × 122 mm

Paper on boards, chromolithographed (with same illustrations on
upper and lower), title on spine.
Private Collection

Bible Pictures & Stories
Partridge, n.d. (inscribed 1886)
215 × 170 mm

Paper on boards printed by chromolithography in brown, blue, red,
green and yellow, on upper, spine
and lower.
Collection the late Percival Hinton

A Story of a Birthday
Miss H. M. Burnside
Illustrations by Alfred W. Cooper,
engraved and printed by Edmund
Evans
S.P.C.K., n.d. [1887]
219 × 176 mm

Cream paper on boards ('engraved
and printed by Edmund Evans'
although the illustration on the front
and those inside appear to be lithographed).
Private Collection

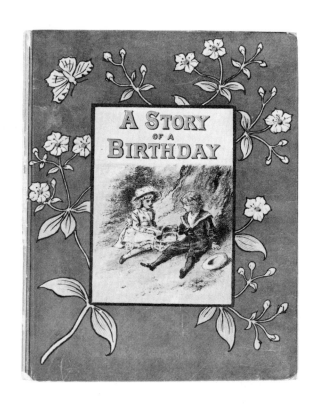

The Book of Birds
E. C. Phillips [Mrs Horace B. Looker]
Griffith Farran, n.d. (advertisement
at back dated 1892)
245 × 192 mm

Paper on boards, chromolithographed by Aug. Karrer, Weimar.
Private Collection

Amusing Pictures
Verses by Constance M. Lowe
Illustrated by E. S. Hardy
Ernest Nister, n.d. (inscribed 1900)
250 × 192 mm

Paper on boards, chromolithographed in Bavaria, green cloth spine.
Every colour plate is 'slatted' and on
pulling a tab a second picture is
'magically' provided.
Private Collection

Aunt Louisa's First Book for Children
Frederick Warne, n.d. (coins dated
1902, p.85)
240 × 200 mm

Paper on boards, chromolithographed probably in Germany. The
illustrations inside (all from wood or
line block, in black and white) include
drawings by Louis Wain.
Private Collection

The Children's Friend, vol. XLI
S. W. Partridge, 1901
235 × 175 mm

Paper on boards, upper cover
chromolithographed, lower cover
with advertisements of Cadbury's
Cocoa and Pear's Soap, with imprint
of Hazell, Watson & Viney, green
cloth spine. The illustrations inside
include half-tone blocks (recently
invented) of photographs and wash
drawings.
Private Collection

The British Workman, vol. XLII
S. W. Partridge, 1896
372 × 275 mm

Paper on boards, cloth spine. Pictorial chromolithographed cover: the whole book printed by Hazell, Watson & Viney. An illustrated article on how this publication was produced contains the statement 'The British Workman is not simply an organ of Temperance, though that always has been, and always will be, in the forefront of its programme.' These annuals were illustrated and produced to a very high standard.
Private Collection

The British Workman, vol. XLV
S W. Partridge, 1899
372 × 275 mm

Paper on boards, pictorial chromo-lithographed cover, cloth spine.
Private Collection

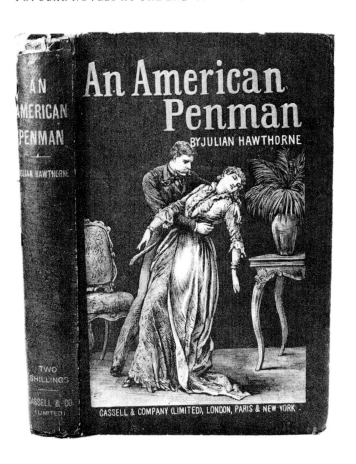

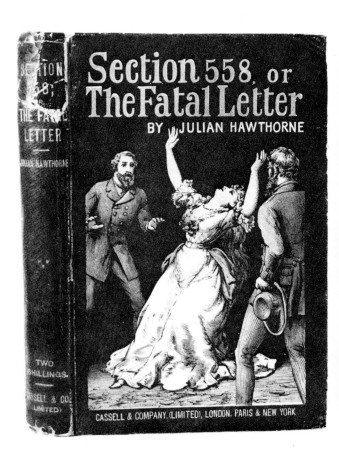

An American Penman
Julian Hawthorne
Cassell, n.d. [*c*.1888]
189 × 125 mm

Cream or yellow paper on boards,
printed in blue, red and green. Sold
at 2*s*. The straight leaves of the potted
fern were, perhaps, easier to engrave
than an aspidistra.

Section 558, or The Fatal Letter
Julian Hawthorne
Cassell, n.d. [*c*.1888]
189 × 125 mm

Cream or yellow paper on boards,
printed in blue, red and green. Uni-
form with *An American Penman.*

The Last Stroke
Lawrence L. Lynch
Ward, Lock, n.d. [1890s]
190 × 120 mm

Paper on boards chromolithographed in Holland in four colours,
red cloth spine blocked in gold.

La Tribu d'Isidore
Victor Joze
Paris, Société de la Librairie Française,
Antony et cie, 1897
186 × 120 mm

Paper (imitation vellum) covers
printed lithographically in colours
from original lithograph by Toulouse
Lautrec. Lautrec had already drawn
the cover for Joze's earlier novel
Babylon d'allemagne, 1894.
*The Houghton Library, Harvard
University Department of Printing and
Graphic Arts*

Les Courtes Joies
Julien Sermet
Paris, Joubert, 1897
185 × 120 mm

Paper (imitation vellum) covers
printed lithographically in colours
from original lithograph by Toulouse
Lautrec.
*The Houghton Library, Harvard
University Department of Printing and
Graphic Arts*

Sir Walter Scott and his Country
Handasyde
Edinburgh, R. Grant & Son;
London, R. Brimley Johnson
MDCCCCIII
150 × 115 mm

Grey paper on boards printed in grey
on upper cover only. Spine of paper
(imitation vellum) printed with title
drawn in grey. The design, in the
William Nicholson-Beggarstaff style,
is by Joseph W. Simpson, who also
designed covers for the Edinburgh
publisher T. N. Foulis. Printed in
Edinburgh by Turnbull & Spears.

An Almanac of Twelve Sports
William Nicholson, words by
Rudyard Kipling
Heinemann, 1898
318 × 252 mm

Paper on boards, printed in black,
brown and yellow on upper, black,
brown and green on the lower, cloth
spine. An example of the return of
style and good design that happened
in the nineties.

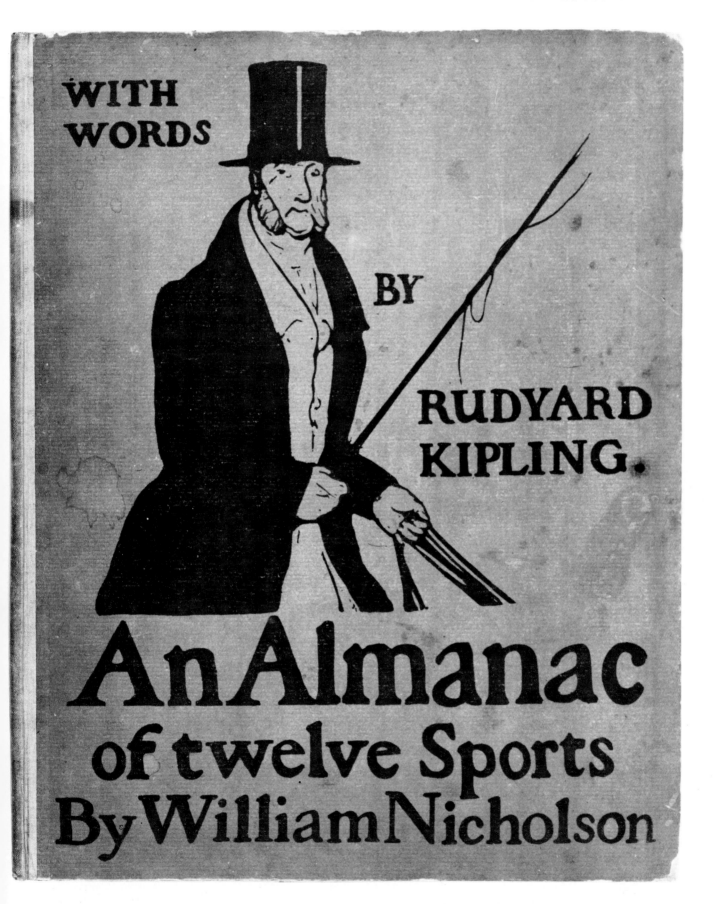

Old English Songs and Dances
Decorated by W. Graham Robertson
Longmans, 1902
400 × 285 mm

Paper on boards, printed in black, grey, grey-green, terracotta, and plum. W. Graham Robertson, who was influenced by William Nichol- son, drew the frontispiece illustration for the first edition of *The Wind in the Willows*. This book was printed by the firm of Edmund Evans.

Private Collection

Index

Bold figures denote illustrations